WORKBOOK

FOR

PISTON/DEVOTO

Harmony

FIFTH EDITION

BY

ARTHUR JANNERY

WESTFIELD STATE COLLEGE

W·W·Norton & Company

New York · London

ISBN 0-393-95484-6

W. W. Norton & Company, Inc., 500 Fifth Avenue, New York, N. Y. 10110
W. W. Norton & Company Ltd., 37 Great Russell Street, London WC1B 3NU

2 3 4 5 6 7 8 9 0

Contents

Foreword

This edition of the *Workbook* is designed to accompany Piston's *Harmony,* Fifth Edition, as revised by Mark DeVoto, and to supplement it where necessary. Because most students will have had previous training in written theory, and some a good deal of it, "where necessary" takes in a lot of territory. Some of you will welcome the persistent drill of fundamentals that this *Workbook* provides; many will profit from the systematic reviews; still others may wish to concentrate on the composition exercises; everyone, it is hoped, will benefit from even greater exposure to a diversity of styles and compositions.

Given the wide differences in musical background of beginning harmony students today, it was felt that a separate volume of exercises, focused especially on the first fifteen text chapters, would be the best place to accommodate individual needs. The necessary flexibility could not have been incorporated into the main text without making it much larger than it already is.

The basic organization of this *Workbook* is straightforward. Each of the fifteen units matches a corresponding chapter of the main text. Within each unit there are five sections. The categories are:

A. A list of *Words and Ideas* to define. All of these references may be found in the corresponding chapter of the text and may be looked up in the Index.

B. *Exercises.* For the most part, these are drills that will require a sort of mental calisthenics on your part. They are to be done by concentrated effort, striving for accuracy and speed.

C. *Analysis.* In the early units, these analytical exercises will help you develop basic skills that are not discussed at great length in the text, but that you will find valuable for harmonic analysis. In the first few units, a system is developed involving graphic representation by which you learn to record the data resulting from your analytical efforts.

D. *Composition Activities.* This is a special category designed to appeal to your creative instincts. You will be called upon to utilize the principles covered in each chapter in a personal, highly individualized manner. Those of you who have not composed before are prime candidates for these activities, since they can introduce you, very gently, to a new world of creativity. As in all original work, the honest opinions of your teacher and fellow students can be of invaluable assistance.

E. *Self Tests.* These brief verbal summaries of each chapter's contents are useful for memorization and spot-checking information. The answers to the Self Tests are found in Appendix I.

The Anthology: New to this edition, the Anthology was designed to meet the needs and interests of the entering undergraduate music major and minor. Through this far-ranging and varied collection of musical bits and pieces, you are offered the unique opportunity to realize concepts and principles of theory through working them out in real music, not in specially manufactured exercises. The selections in this Anthology go somewhat beyond the chronological limits of the period generally associated with common practice, but the music lends itself perfectly well to the conventions delineated in the text.

In the Analysis sections, you will be regularly called upon to work with specific pieces from the Anthology and perform specific tasks. However, not all of the selections included in the Anthology are utilized in this way. Both instructor and student are invited to use the music in the Anthology in as many ways as prove helpful for the enhancement and illumination of the text.

We have not provided exercises in this *Workbook* for Chapters 16 onward, because we are convinced that the need for this kind of reinforcement is greatest in the earlier stages of study. This is, after all, a workbook; it is designed to help you work directly and abundantly with the material: to get your hands dirty with notes, so to speak. The kind of experience you acquire here may only be a beginning, but it will be a beginning that amounts to much more than memorization of rules; it will involve the things that composers think about and analytical skills that are basic to the musicians' craft. Those, in turn, will provide the kind of insight into music that will serve you well both as performer and listener.

Acknowledgments

I wish to thank the many students who have been in my music theory sequence and composition classes over the past twenty years; the insight they have provided has been critical in the development of this *Workbook*. Recent graduate students Alice Anderson and Thomas Scavone have interacted with some of the material in its early stages and brought forth valuable suggestions for improvements.

Thanks to my colleagues, particularly to Andy Jaffe and Alice Spatz, who contributed their creative efforts to the Anthology, and to Floyd Corson and Daniel Koury for their review of materials of the Anthology, and for other assistance.

The staff of W. W. Norton & Company deserves much praise—especially Claire Brook, Music Editor, for her assistance in the creation of this new edition.

My family has provided very special support. Thank you to my wife Marti, to Jonathan, Beth, and Melanie.

Finally, I am very much in debt to Mark DeVoto for his excellent work, which is now manifest in the Fifth Edition of Piston's *Harmony*.

Arthur Jannery
Westfield, Massachusetts
September 1986

Scales and Intervals

SECTION A

Words and Ideas

Define in your own words:

interval	harmonic interval	melodic interval
diatonic scale	scale	chromatic scale
half step	octave	circle of fifths
scale degrees	I, II, III, etc.	tonic
supertonic	mediant	subdominant
dominant	submediant	leading tone
subtonic	general interval name	specific interval name
major interval	perfect interval	minor interval
augmented interval	diminished interval	semitone
compound intervals	harmonic inversion	complementary intervals
enharmonic intervals		

SECTION B

Exercises

Intervals Measured by Scales

1. Add tones a half step *below* and *above* each given tone, as in the Example.

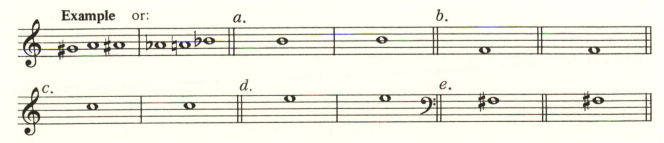

2. Using appropriate accidental signs (sharps for ascending motion, flats for descending motion), and without altering the first pitch, transform each of the following examples into chromatic lines.

3. Fill in the notes necessary to create ascending or descending chromatic scales between the given pitches. (Remember that *as a rule* sharps are used when the scale ascends, flats when it descends.)

Diatonic Scales

4. Add tones that will be both a whole step and a letter name above and below the given tone (see the Example).

5. Identify each pair of tones as either a half step (½) or a whole step (1) apart.

6. Write out the intervallic series of whole step—whole step—and half step (1–1–½), ascending, starting on each of the given tones. Label the intervals as shown in the Example.

7. Using each of the given tones as a tonic or as a dominant note, write the three ascending major scale degrees that should follow (1–1–½).

Tonic is given:

Dominant is given:

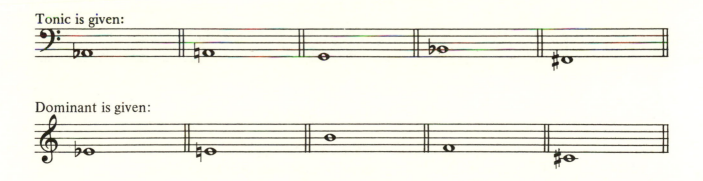

8. In the following ascending and descending scale segments, mark each pair of tones that are a half step apart, as shown in the Example. Determine the keynote of the major scale within each line and circle it.

3

9. Write the signatures for the following major keys.

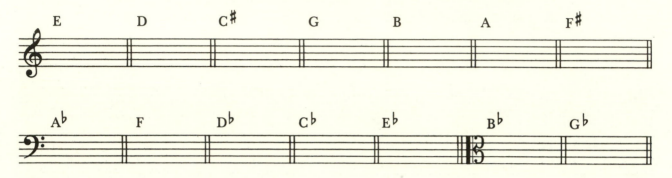

10. Indicate the names of the major keys that correspond to the following signatures.

Scale Degrees

11. In each of the following excerpts, circle the noteheads that are tonics, subdominants, dominants, or supertonics. Put a diagonal line through each leading-tone notehead. Circle all submediants and mediants in a different color.

a.   Kuhlau, *Sonatina,* Op. 55, No. 1

b.

Andante mosso

Verdi, *Lu traviata*

Ad - di - o___ del pas - sa - to___ bei___

c.

Reichardt, *Jägers Nachtlied*

Slowly

Im Fel - de schleich' ich still und wild, lausch' mit dem Feu - er - rohr;

12. Fill in the blanks below.

   a. A is the supertonic in the key of _____.

   b. B♭ is the submediant in the key of _____.

   c. C♯ is the dominant in the key of _____.

   d. D is the leading tone in the key of _____.

   e. E♭ is the tonic in the key of _____.

   f. F♯ is the subdominant in the key of _____.

   g. G is the mediant in the key of _____.

Intervals and Their Classification

13. Give the general name for each of the following harmonic intervals.

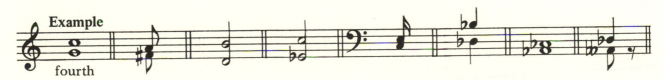

Example

fourth

14. Each of the following groups contains intervals of the same general type, but with different specific names. Give both the general and specific names.

15. Give the general name for each of the following melodic intervals:

16. In each of the following, the lower note is the keynote. Fill in the interval with notes of the major scale. Indicate whether or not the upper note is a degree of this scale. Also give the general name of each interval.

17. Provide the specific interval names for all the examples in numbers 13, 15, and 16 above.

18. Give both general and specific names of each of the harmonic intervals below.

19. Give the general and specific names for each of the following melodic intervals.

Compound Intervals

20. Rewrite the following compound intervals naming each, as in the example.

Inversion of Intervals

21. Invert each interval as suggested by the example and label each set of complementary intervals.

Enharmonic Intervals

22. Write an enharmonic equivalent for each given interval, as in the example below.

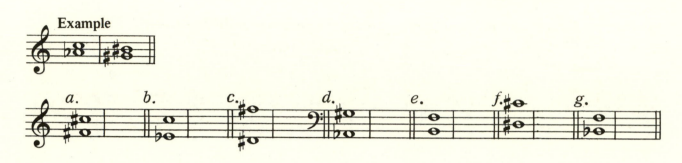

SECTION C

Analysis

1. For each of the following, provide the key, the key signature, and write out the scale implicit in the excerpt.

Example Schubert, *Impromptu,* Op. 90, No. 3

G♭ major

a.

b.

Beethoven, *Alla Ingharese, Quasi un Capriccio* (The Rage Over a Lost Penny, Vented in a Caprice), Op. 129

c.

Beethoven, *Sonata,* Op. 7, IV

2. For each selection from the Anthology listed below, give the key, key signature, and appropriate scale on the staff provided. (N.B.: The key signature does not always match the key being used, especially in a section within a composition.)

   a. 1b: J. C. Bach, *Husar Regiment of Württemberg,* mm. 5–11

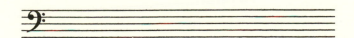

b. 4: J. S. Bach, *Sleepers, Awake,* mm. 9–11

c. 15b: L. Couperin, *Double on Rigaudon,* mm. 1–5

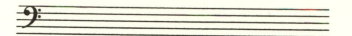

d. 13: Corelli, Sonata, mm. 22–27

SECTION D

Composition Activities

In all your composition activities, make every effort to think of your work in terms of how it might be performed. To this end, try to learn how different instruments and voices sound in their different ranges and combinations, and what they can do best. Such things are covered in detail in an orchestration course, but you will find it very helpful to acquire an elementary knowledge of instruments and voices as you work on your assignments here.

There is a list of ranges and a transposition chart in the Appendices that will serve as a convenient beginning. But most important of all is listening to the actual sound of instruments and voices often enough to become familiar with their qualities. In that way you will learn of their technical possibilities, their musical suitabilities, what they cannot do, and what they ought not be asked to do. Therefore, try out what you write or have it tried out for you. That is the best way to discover, for example, that a lot of fast notes over a wide range played brilliantly on a cello will probably sound awful on a trombone; or, on the other hand, that an ordinary chordal passage for strings can gain a great deal when played by a brass ensemble.

Professional composers are often asked whether or not it is advisable to compose at the piano. The answer is, of course, that there *is* no answer to that question. Some composers do and some don't. Certainly, the piano can be a great help at any stage in the compositional process, but it should never become a substitute for *hearing* in your head what you see on the page. Try to free yourself from dependency on the piano; this is a good goal to strive for in your harmony studies.

In the early units of this *Workbook,* we have provided blank staves for writing out your compositions. As the assignments become longer and more complicated, you will find a music notebook with ten or twelve staves printed on each page indispensable for sketching out and making fair copies of your original pieces.

1. Write a stately melody for one of the solo brass instruments mentioned below, using the three notes indicated and no others in your composition. (You may use additional octave equivalents of any of the three pitches, provided they are in the instrument's practical range.) Indicate all dynamics, phrasing, and articulation, by means of appropriate markings.

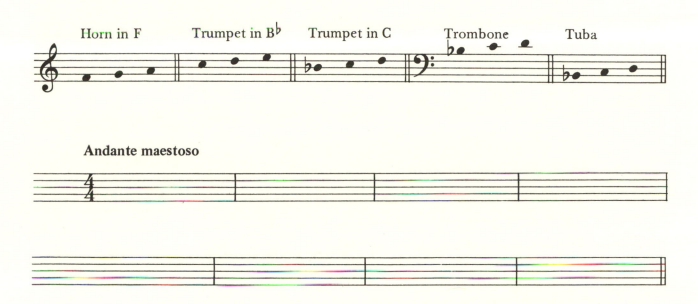

2. Write a lively melody for clarinet or bassoon. Use the scale fragment given below with octave equivalents within the instrument's range, if you wish. Indicate dynamics, phrasing, and articulation.

3. Write a lyric melody for muted cello, based entirely on the following fragment:

Andante cantabile

4. Compose a melody in F major for the following text, using the rhythm and meter given:

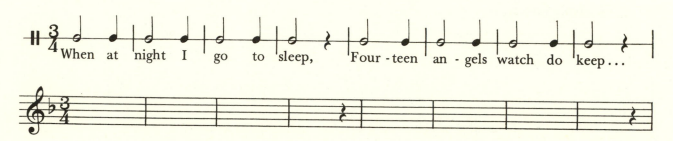

When at night I go to sleep, Four-teen an-gels watch do keep...

This will not be a complete composition; create a feeling of wanting to go on at the end. Choose a suitable tempo and dynamics.

5. Now write another setting of the text above, using the same rhythm and meter but otherwise completely different. Use the key of D major; choose your own dynamics and tempo.

6. For a final setting of the same text, you may choose your own rhythm, meter, tempo, and major key. You may also use two or more pitches for each syllable of the text, where you feel that such a treatment is appropriate.

Self Test

1. The sound that is almost an exact duplicate of a given pitch, either twelve half steps or seven letter names higher or lower, is the _____ .

2. A diatonic scale will have _____ different tones.

3. The chromatic scale has _____ more tones than the diatonic scale.

4. The major scale has the following succession of whole and half steps: _____ _____ _____ _____ _____ _____ _____ .

5. Another name for "keynote" is _____ .

6. The names of the scale degrees are: I _____ , II _____ , III _____ , IV _____ , V _____ , VI _____ , and VII _____ .

7. Distances between pitches are called _____ .

8. The general names of intervals are determined by counting the _____ between tones.

9. The specific names of intervals are found by noting the correspondence between the upper tone and the _____ scale of the lower tone.

10. If the two tones of an interval are successive, that is, they follow each other in time, the interval is called a _____ interval.

11. If the tones sound together it is called a _____ interval.

12. Thirds may be either _____ , _____ , _____ , or _____ .

13. Unisons, octaves, fourths, and fifths may be _____ , _____ , or _____ .

14. An interval larger than an octave is called a _____ interval.

15. Intervals that sound relatively stable are referred to as _____ intervals.

16. Those intervals whose sounds are relatively restless and in need of resolution to a stable interval are called _____ intervals.

17. The consonant intervals are the _____ , _____ , _____ , _____ , _____ , _____ , _____ , and sometimes the _____ .

18. The major and minor seconds and sevenths are _____ intervals.

19. Augmented and diminished intervals are considered to be _____ intervals.

20. A major interval becomes _____ when inverted.

21. An augmented interval becomes _____ when inverted.

22. The inversion of any perfect interval will be _____.

23. A seventh when inverted becomes a _____.

24. A major third inverts to become a _____.

25. The following intervals: are called _____ of each other.

26. The order of sharps in the key signature of seven sharps, read from left to right,

is _____, _____, _____, _____, _____, _____, and _____.

27. The order of flats in the key signature of seven flats, read from left to right,

is _____, _____, _____, _____, _____, _____, and _____.

28. The keynotes of the major keys in order from one sharp through seven sharps

are _____, _____, _____, _____, _____, _____, and _____.

29. The keynotes of the major keys in order from one flat through seven flats

are _____, _____, _____, _____, _____, _____, and _____.

Triads

SECTION A

Words and Ideas

Define in your own words:

chord   triad   root
third   fifth   major triads
minor triads   augmented triads   diminished triads
root position   first inversion   second inversion
consonant intervals   dissonant intervals   consonant chords
dissonant chords   four-part writing   SATB
doubling   spacing   close position
open position

SECTION B

Exercises

Chord Factors

1. Each of the following musical fragments is based on a triad. As demonstrated in the example below, rearrange the tones into a triad in close root-position form. (Note: two of the examples contain an extra note that you may omit from your reduction.)

Triads on the Scale Degrees

2. Write out the triads of the following major keys. As in Example 2–2 of your text (page 13), label each chord with a roman numeral.

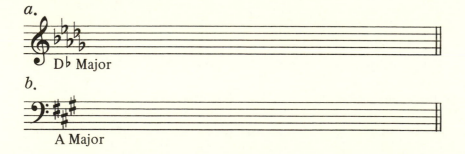

Kinds of Triads

3. Add a major third and a perfect fifth above each given tone to form major triads.

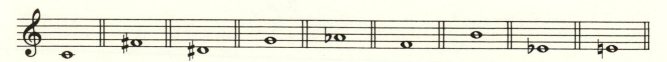

4. Lower the third of each of the given major triads to transform them into minor triads.

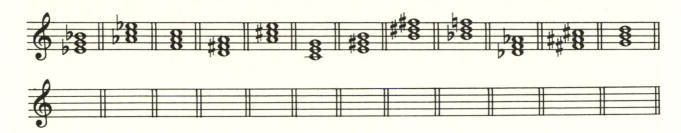

5. Add a minor third and perfect fifth above each given tone to form minor triads.

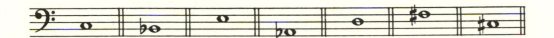

6. Identify each of the triads below as major, minor, augmented, or diminished.

7. Construct major, minor, augmented, and diminished triads, in that order, above each of the given notes.

Example

Inversions

8. Below each triad, indicate $\frac{5}{3}$ (for root position), $\frac{6}{3}$ (first inversion), or $\frac{6}{4}$ (second inversion).

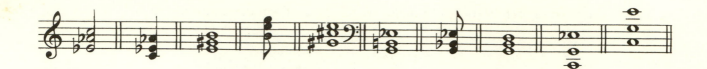

9. Rewrite the given triads in the positions indicated, as in the example below.

Consonant and Dissonant Intervals

10. Turn back to page 5 of this *Workbook.* In questions 13, 14, and 18, circle all the dissonant intervals you can find.

11. Circle all consonant triads in questions 8 and 9 above.

Triads of the Major Mode

12. Write out all the triads in the major scales with the following key signatures, indicating the quality of each (use M for major, m for minor, + for augmented, and − for diminished).

Doubling

13. Below are chords in four parts (SATB). For the moment, doubling the root is the correct procedure to follow. Fill in the noteheads of the doubled pitch in each chord and circle each chord that has a doubled root.

Spacing

14. Each triad below has a spacing problem. Locate the problem and indicate which pair of voices is involved (S–A or A–T).

15. Rewrite all the triads in question 14 to demonstrate good spacing.

SECTION C

Analysis

We will use the following procedure to record the results of your analyses throughout this *Workbook:*

    1. Use a bass-clef staff.
    2. Provide key and time signatures and tempo indications, when given.
    3. Provide the root pitch of each chord, using the following symbols to indicate triad quality: M = major   m = minor
                                 + = augmented   − = diminished

4. Use arabic numbers to indicate position of each triad, i.e.:

   $\frac{5}{3}$ = root position (to be omitted after this unit. When there is no arabic numbers, root position will be assumed.)

   $\frac{6}{3}$ = first inversion (in later units, 6 alone will suffice)

   $\frac{6}{4}$ = second inversion

5. Use arabic numbers to indicate position in seventh chords, as follows:

   7 = root position

   $\frac{6}{5}$ = first inversion

   $\frac{4}{3}$ = second inversion

   $\frac{4}{2}$ = third or last inversion

6. Use upper-case roman numerals to indicate the function of each triad or seventh chord in relation to the prevailing key.

7. Use "?" instead of a roman numeral for chords you have not yet studied. Later, you will not need this symbol. Meanwhile, it will be used primarily for chords that include chromatic pitches.

Note: This system does not employ symbols to indicate the duration of each sonority. Relative duration may be inferred by the position of the root pitch within the measure and by its relation to other root pitches and barlines.

1. Analyze each of the following excerpts, recording the results of your analysis on the blank staffs provided.

Example

a.

20

b.

c.

Wagner, *Tannhäuser*

2. Apply the same procedure to the following excerpts from the Anthology. Record your answers on the blank staves provided below.

a. 14: F. Couperin, *Le Tic-Toc-Choc,* mm. 1–9

b. 20: Gilbert and Sullivan, *"The Flowers that Bloom in the Spring,"* mm. 5–8

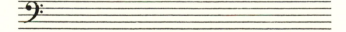

c. 18: Donizetti, Recitativo from *Betly,* mm. 1–7

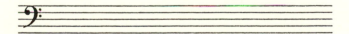

d. 23: Handel, *Joy to the World,* the entire piece.

Composition Activities

1. Write a phrase four measures long based entirely on tonic harmony in F major. Use the following pattern for piano to accompany a legato melody in the low register of a bass instrument. The tempo should be Lento or Andante.

2. Using the same accompaniment, write a lyrical melody in moderate tempo for a treble instrument.

3. Write two four-measure phrases for trumpet and piano using the given measure as a model for the accompaniment. Use only tonic harmony throughout. Indicate all dynamic, phrasing, and articulation markings in both parts.

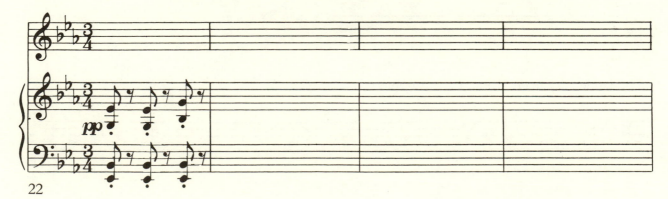

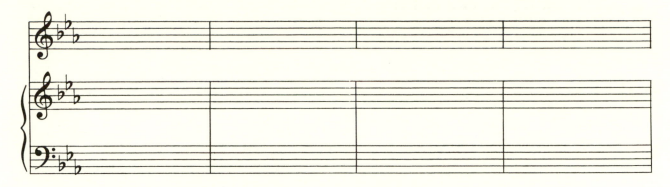

4. Go through the Anthology and find examples of *left-hand* patterns that unmistakably project a single root-position harmony in a way that is characteristically pianistic, such as the well-known oom-pah-pah waltz accompaniment:

or a rolling arpeggiation:

Now compose three such left-hand patterns, each four measures long, similar to the ones you just found, and add a suitable right-hand melody. Your accompaniment should outline a single root-position chord throughout.

Self Test

1. The simultaneous sounding of two or more harmonic intervals is called a _____ .

2. The _____ is the basic chord, built of three tones.

3. The triad results from the superposition of two _____ .

4. The factors of any triad are referred to as the _____ , the _____ , and the _____ .

5. The four basic types of triads are major _____ , _____ , _____ , and _____ .

6. Between its root and its other factors, a major triad always has the intervals of a _____ third and a _____ fifth.

7. The _____ triad always has a minor third and a diminshed fifth between the root and the other tones.

8. The augmented triad has a _____ and an _____ fifth between the root and the other tones.

9. In what ways are major and minor triads alike? In what ways are they different?

   _____

   _____

10. When the root is *not* the lowest tone, the chord is said to be _____ .

11. The _____ of the triad is in the lowest voice when the chord is in second inversion.

12. When the third of the triad is the lowest tone, the chord is said to be in _____ inversion.

13. The _____ and _____ triads are consonant.

14. The _____ and _____ triads are dissonant.

15. In any major key, major triads are found on the _____, _____, and _____ degrees.

16. On II, III, and VI in any major key the triads are _____ .

17. The triad on VII of any major key is always _____ .

18. An augmented triad _____ available diatonically in any major key.

is/is not

19. The names customarily applied to the individual parts in four-part writing

are: _____, _____, _____, and _____.

20. In four-part writing, the duplication of one of the triadic factors in order to obtain a

fourth part is called _____.

21. The _____ is usually selected to be doubled in a root-position triad.

22. The leading tone usually _____ doubled, even when the VII triad is used.

is/is not

23. The most common arrangement of the notes in an SATB construct is to have

the _____ intervals on the bottom, with the _____ intervals toward

the top.

Harmonic Progression in the Major Mode: Rules of Voice Leading

SECTION A

Words and Ideas

Define in your own words:

harmonic progression	strong progression	weak progression
Rules of Thumb	linear movement	common tone
conjunct motion	disjunct motion	Rules of Motion
contrary motion	oblique motion	similar motion
parallel motion	direct motion	hidden octaves (or 5ths)
direct octaves (or 5ths)	leading-tone resolution	tritone
overlapping	crossing	

SECTION B

Exercises

Table of Root Progressions

1. Having become familiar with the Table of Root Progressions in Chapter 3 of your text, you can now provide the root and label of the chord most likely to follow the chords indicated below.

B♭ Major: V   II   VI   III   VII   IV   I

D Major: I   IV   VII   III   VI   II   V

Connection of Chords: Two Rules of Thumb

Note: Unless specific instructions are given to the contrary, all the exercises in this section are to be worked out in the same rhythm as the given notes.

2. Following Rule of Thumb 1 precisely, work out each of the progressions below in four parts. Be very careful about doubling and spacing. Indicate the key of each progression and provide a root analysis by adding the appropriate roman numerals.

Example

D: V I

3. Complete each of the following in four parts, but do not retain the common tone in the same voice. Be careful to avoid prohibited motion in voice leading, and be sure to observe proper doubling. Indicate the key and provide a root analysis for each progression.

4. The most frequently used harmonic progression whose chords do not share common tones is IV–V. Work out the following examples in four parts, applying Rule of Thumb 2.

Example

C: IV V   IV V   IV V   IV V   IV V

5. A usual exception to Rule of Thumb 2 is the V–VI progression, especially when the leading tone in the soprano resolves up by step to the tonic. Work out the following examples in the spaces provided.

Example

F: V VI   V VI   V VI   V VI   V VI

Conjunct and Disjunct Melodic Motion

6. Return to exercises 2 through 5 above and indicate next to each progression
whether the melodic motion you have employed is primarily conjunct or disjunct.

Rules of Motion

7. Mark each of the fragments below according to the type of motion observed. Use
the following key:

        C = contrary motion   S = similar motion
        O = oblique motion   P = parallel motion

8. In one of the fragments above there are parallels that should be avoided. What are
the parallel intervals? Circle that example.

The Direct Octave and Fifth

Note: The rules governing direct motion to a fifth or octave distinguish between two situations: (1) when both voices skip, and (2) where one voice skips and the other steps.

Skipping in the same direction in both voices to an octave or fifth is to be *avoided*.

Direct motion to an octave or fifth with one voice stepping is always *permitted* between any pair of voices, *except* when the soprano (if involved) skips.
Not permitted:

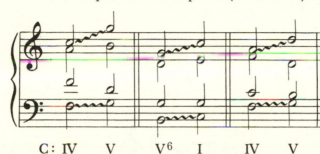

C: IV   V   V⁶   I   IV   V

9. With these constraints in mind, examine the progressions below and determine what types of direct motion to an octave or fifth they contain. Where the motion is incorrect, mark it with wavy lines; where it is correct, mark it with dotted lines.

Example

C: IV   I

10. Rewrite the progressions repeated below, avoiding incorrect motion to a fifth or octave.

29

Treatment of the Leading Tone

11. Circle the leading tone within each pair of chords below. Then connect it to the next tone in the same voice to observe its resolution. The leading tone usually ascends by step, but may descend when it occurs in an inner voice.

C: V   I

Overlapping and Crossing

12. Renotate the notes that cross as in the example.

13. Locate the pair of overlapping voices in each progression. Circle those that are acceptable.

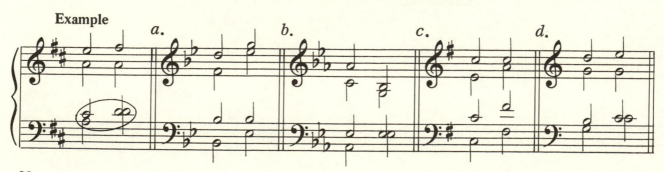

Similar Motion of Four Voices

14. Rewrite each of the progressions below, avoiding similar motion in all the voices.

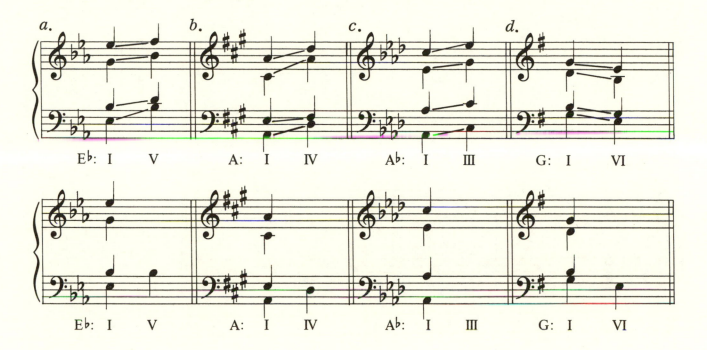

Eb: I V   A: I IV   Ab: I III   G: I VI

Supplementary Exercises

The following exercises, a bit longer than those we have done, are derived from the literature. Work them out in four parts; label all keys and chords.

a. **Allegretto**   Schubert, *Impromptu,* Op. 90, No. 4

b.   Haydn, *Symphony No. 94* ("Surprise"), II (adapted)

   Andante

Kuhlau, *Sonatina,* Op. 55, No. 4, II (adapted)

Andante con espressione

p sostenuto

d.

Beethoven, *Sonata,* Op. 13 ("Pathétique"), II (adapted)

Adagio cantabile

e.

Dvořák, *Slavonic Dance,* Op. 46, No. 5 (adapted)

Allegro vivace

SECTION C

Analysis

1. Examine the excerpts that follow. Complete a key–chord analysis according to the procedures established on pages 19ff. Circle all nonchord tones on the music itself. (Nonchord, or nonharmonic, tones are melodic tones that do not belong to the chord with which they are sounded.) Record the results of your analysis on the blank staff below each excerpt.

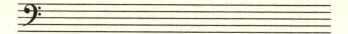

2. Now follow the same procedure for the following Anthology excerpts:

a. 24: Handel, "He Was Despised" from *Messiah,* mm. 1–8

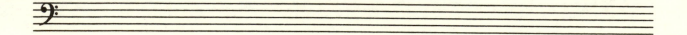

b. 26: Haydn, *Twelve German Dances,* No. 2, entire piece

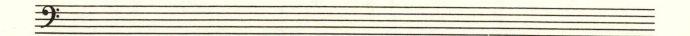

c. 26: Haydn, *Twelve German Dances,* No. 3, entire piece

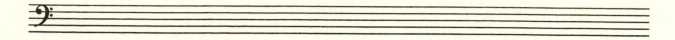

d. 26: Haydn, *Twelve German Dances,* No. 4, entire piece

Composition Activities

1. Extend the pattern given in the first measure below through three measures of sub-dominant and tonic triads. (Don't change the spacing; apply Rule of Thumb 1 to obtain minimal motion. The lowest voice is to be considered a textural duplication of the bass line throughout this five-part pattern.)

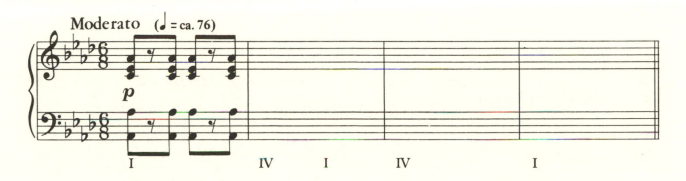

2. Continue the accompanimental pattern of the piano excerpt given below, inventing an original continuation of the melody appropriate to the harmony. Follow the chord pattern indicated. The extension of the melody should have essentially the same note values as in the given measure; this will lend rhythmic unity to the passage.

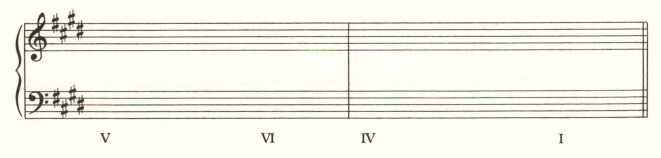

3. Work out the following in rhythmic unison, according to the rhythm and root progressions given. Move the upper parts up or down fairly freely as you wish, but keep them always in close position. Choose a suitable tempo and dynamics. Score for three clarinets and bass clarinet.

4. Using the given measure as a beginning, write several extensions according to the chords and rhythms indicated.

5. Compose a fanfare, Maestoso, for two trumpets and two trombones, on the harmonic pattern indicated below. The rhythm will be your own choice, but all parts must proceed in rhythmic unison.

SECTION E

Self Test

1. Harmonic progressions may be classified according to the relative distances between the _____ of the triads involved.

2. The harmonic progression II–V is an example of a root succession that is _____ used.
   frequently/infrequently

3. The progression from II to V would be classified as a _____ progression.
   strong/weak

4. The harmonic progression involving root succession with movement up a third is usually considered to be _____.
   strong/weak

5. Root successions by upward step, upward perfect fifth, or upward perfect fourth are relatively _____ in music.
   common/uncommon

6. Voice leading is the means whereby one chord is _____ to another.

37

7. State Rule of Thumb 1 in your own words. _____

_____

_____

8. What is the common exception to Rule of Thumb 1? _____

_____

9. State Rule of Thumb 2 in your own words. _____

_____

_____

10. What progression is the common exception to Rule of Thumb 2? _____

_____

11. On occasion, it is possible or even desirable to omit the _____ of a triad, and to _____ its root.

12. It is generally undesirable to omit the _____ of a triad, because it leaves the open sound of the _____ .

13. Does the change of position of a chord, without other intervening chords sounding, constitute a harmonic progression? _____

14. Movement of a line by step is called _____ melodic motion.

15. Disjunct Melodic Motion involves motion by _____ .

16. The types of Motion that may be found between two voices are _____, _____, and _____ motion.

17. An octave or perfect fifth *is not* usually approached by similar motion with skips in both voices _____ (true or false).

18. Direct fifths and octaves are permitted only in certain instances. These are: _____

_____

_____

19. What is a tritone? Why is it so called? _____

20. Define overlapping voices. _____

_____

The Minor Mode

SECTION A

Words and Ideas

Define in your own words

natural minor   **harmonic minor**   **augmented second**
melodic minor   **relative minor**   **parallel modes**
minor scale signatures

SECTION B

Exercises

Relative Scales
(see Chapter Five)

1. Assume that each note given below is the keynote of a major scale. Write in the keynote of its relative minor.

Maj. min.

2. The keynotes to various minor scales are written below. Write in the keynote of the relative major scale for each.

min. Maj.

3. Name the natural minor scale indicated by the following key signatures. Write in your answers below each key signature.

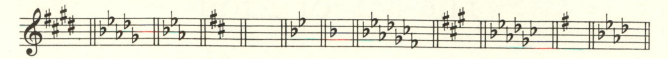

4. Name the major scale indicated by each signature in question 3. Write in the answer above the signatures.

Natural Minor Scales

5. Circle each pair of successive tones that form a half step in each of the following scale segments. Then determine the particular natural minor scale that is hidden in each succession and identify it by putting an X through the keynote.

6. Without altering the initial keynotes, add the accidentals to the following scales that will transform them into natural minor scales.

7. Write out natural minor scales for the keynotes indicated below. Use accidental signs rather than key signatures. Write letter names below each note and indicate where half steps occur above the appropriate pairs of notes.

40

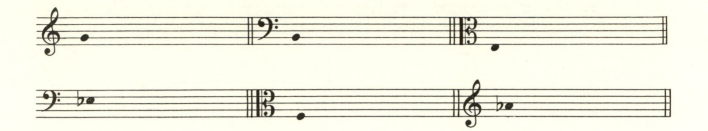

Melodic Minor Scales

9. Write the ascending and descending forms of the melodic minor scales for the given keynotes. Do not use key signatures, but write in accidentals where required.

Harmonic Minor Scales

8. Write out the harmonic minor scales for the keynotes indicated below and complete the exercise exactly as you did for question 7 above, with one exception: provide the key signatures and write in the accidental for the seventh degree only.

Triads in the Minor Mode

10. Write out the triads found in each harmonic minor scale indicated by the keynotes given below. Label each triad major, minor, augmented, or diminished.

11. In any harmonic minor scale, I and IV are minor triads;

V and VI are major triads;

II and VII are diminished triads;

III is an augmented triad.

Therefore: *a.* the triad C–E♭–G may be found on (for example) __IV__ in __G__ harmonic minor, and on _____ in _____ harmonic minor;

b. the triad C–E–G may be found on _____ in _____ harmonic minor, and on _____ in _____ harmonic minor;

c. the triad C–E–G♯ may be found on _____ in _____ harmonic minor.

d. the triad C–E♭–G♭ is always found on _____ in _____ harmonic minor, and on _____ in _____ harmonic minor.

12. Each of the following triads may be found in more than one harmonic minor scale. Determine the structural type of each triad and name all the scales in which each will be found.

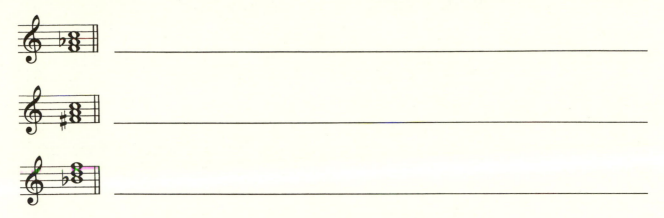

13. Write down the triads indicated, using accidental signs and omitting key signatures. Derive the triads from the harmonic minor scale only.

f: II   V   VII   g: III   VI   II   e: I   IV   VI

bb: I   V   III   f#: IV   V   VI

Harmonic Progression and Voice Leading

14. Provide a four-part harmonization for each of the following bass lines, using root-position triads only, note against note. The seventh degree will be raised in the dominant chords. Be careful to avoid the melodic interval of augmented second.

a.

(freely adapted from Beethoven)

Maestoso

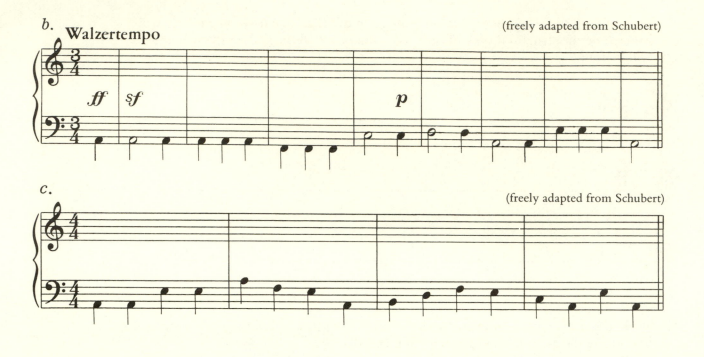

b. **Walzertempo** (freely adapted from Schubert)

c. (freely adapted from Schubert)

Analysis

1. Analyze each of the following excerpts and provide the following:

on the staff above each excerpt the appropriate scale form (i.e., natural, harmonic, or melodic);

on the staff below each excerpt a key–chord analysis using the procedure detailed on pages 19ff.

Mendelssohn, *Violin Concerto*, Op. 64, I

a.

Allegro molto appassionato

Root

Root

(7)   (7)

b.   Purcell, *Dido and Aeneas*

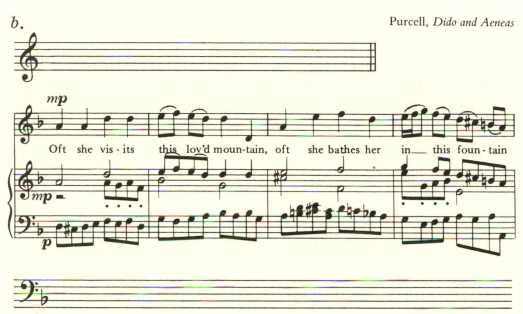

Oft she vis-its   this lov'd moun-tain, oft   she bathes her   in___ this foun-tain

c.   Mozart, *Violin Sonata,* K. 304, I

Allegro

p espress.

d.

2. Analyze the following excerpts from the Anthology in the same way and record your answers on the two staves provided for that purpose.

a. 30: Mozart, *Symphony in G minor,* mm. 1–5

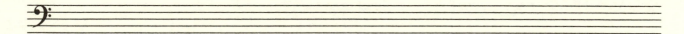

b. 37: Schumann, *The Poor Orphan Child,* No. 6 from *Album for the Young,* Op. 68, mm. 1–8

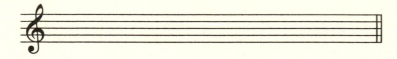

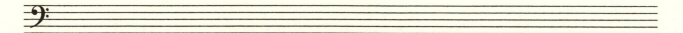

c. 39c: Spatz (arr.), *The Irish Washerwoman,* entire song

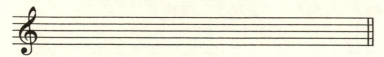

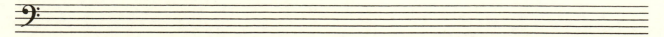

Composition Activities

1. Beginning with the measure given below (borrowed from Schubert), complete one four-measure phrase, using one of three chord progressions indicated. There is to be only one harmony per measure.

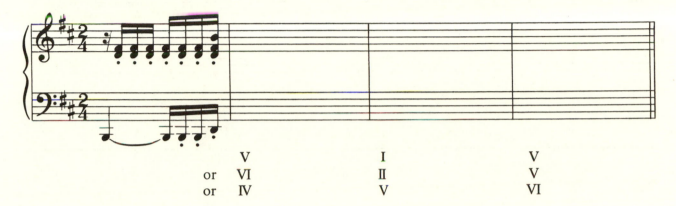

	V	I	V
or	VI	II	V
or	IV	V	VI

2. Write another four-measure phrase, using two harmonies per measure in the last three measures, thus:

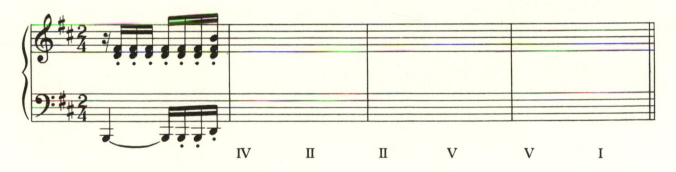

| IV | II | II | V | V | I |

3. Write a slow, mournful melody for solo oboe based entirely on the following scale:

4. Using the following scale as a basis,

compose an original melody in a happy, dancelike mood, for clarinet.

SECTION E

Self Test

1. The letter names of the scale degrees of F minor are: _____, _____, _____, ____, _____, _____, and _____.

2. A natural minor scale has the same signature as its _____ major scale.

3. The keynote of the natural minor is a _____ third _____ than the keynote of its relative major.

4. The keynote of any major scale is a _____ third _____ than the keynote of the natural minor scale with the same key signature.

5. Is it true or false that on occasion all minor scale forms may be found within the same composition, or even within the same section of a composition? _____

6. The particular scale degree that differentiates the natural minor scale from the harmonic minor scale having the same tonic is the _____ degree.

7. The harmonic minor differs from the natural minor in that the _____ degree is _____.

8. The harmonic minor differs from the major scale having the same tonic in its _____ and _____ degrees. These are _____ than in the major.
   _{higher/lower}

9. Compared to the natural minor, the ascending form of the melodic minor on the same keynote has the _____ and _____ degrees _____.

48

10. The descending melodic minor is _____ from the natural minor.
    different/no different

11. If the _____ degree of the major scale is lowered, the scale becomes identical to the melodic minor, ascending.

12. The augmented second, as a melodic interval that is usually avoided, occurs between the _____ and _____, or the _____ and _____ degrees of the harmonic minor scale.

13. In constructing harmony, the _____ form of the minor scale will most frequently be considered.

14. The augmented triad on the mediant degree in the minor mode is _____
    frequently/infrequently
    encountered in music.

15. The principles of voice leading that govern correct harmonic progression and chord connection in the minor mode are _____ those of the major
    essentially the same as/fundamentally different from
    mode.

Tonality and Modality

SECTION A

Words and Ideas

Define in your own words

tonality	tonal system	modality
modal scales	Aeolian	Ionian
Dorian	Phrygian	Lydian
Mixolydian	transposed modes	tonal function
tonal degrees	modal degrees	authentic cadence
tonal strength	musical "words"	modal interchange
mixed modes	the Picardy third	secondary dominant
tonicize	chromaticism	arpeggiation

SECTION B

Exercises

Modal Scales

1. The "diatonic circle" at the top of page 51 is useful in determining the various modal scales. The starting point is indicated for each of the modes, whose intervallic succession is then read in a clockwise direction around the circle.

   Study the diagram carefully, then answer the following questions concerning the pattern of half and whole steps for each mode:

   The pattern of half and whole steps for each mode is:

   a. Ionian mode (major) **Example:** ___1___ ___1___ ___½___ ___1___ ___1___ ___1___ ___½___

   b. Dorian ___ ___ ___ ___ ___ ___ ___

   c. Phrygian ___ ___ ___ ___ ___ ___ ___

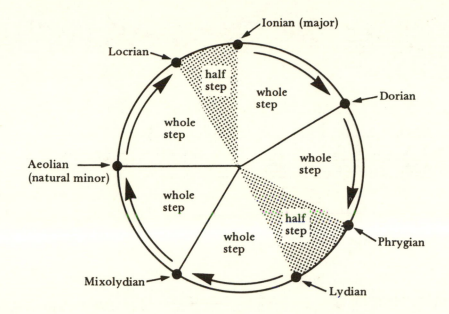

d. Lydian _____ _____ _____ _____ _____ _____ _____ _____

e. Mixolydian _____ _____ _____ _____ _____ _____ _____ _____

f. Aeolian (natural minor) _____ _____ _____ _____ _____ _____ _____ _____

g. Locrian _____ _____ _____ _____ _____ _____ _____ _____

2. Before proceeding with another exercise in modal scales, there are two important points that need to be made:

Modal scales should be recalled in the following "special" order:

1. Ionian (major)

2. Dorian

3. Phrygian

4. Lydian

5. Mixolydian

6. Aeolian (natural minor)

7. Locrian

The arabic numbers that precede the mode names are also an important part of that "special" order, since they may be considered to represent major scale degrees and therefore provide a key to the relationship of the modal scales to the more familiar major scales. Study the example below very carefully. In the space between the staves, name the modes written out on the top line and then write out their equivalents in F major on the lower line provided for that purpose.

C Major

F Major

3. Write out the following modes, starting on C:

Aeolian (or natural minor)   Dorian   Phrygian

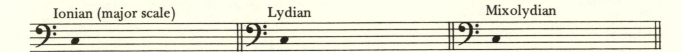

Ionian (major scale)   Lydian   Mixolydian

Compare the scales you have just constructed and answer the following questions:

a. Which degree in Dorian mode differs from the natural minor and in what way?

_____

b. Which degree in Phrygian mode differs from the Aeolian mode and in what way?

_____

c. In what way is the Lydian mode different from the major mode? _____

_____

d. Which degree (or degrees) in Mixolydian mode is different from the major and in what way?

_____

_____

Tonal Functions of the Scale Degrees

4. Name the tonal degrees of the following scales.

   a. F major: _____ _____ _____ _____

   b. E minor: (harmonic)   _____ _____ _____ _____

   c. D major: _____ _____ _____ _____

d. B major:　　　＿＿＿ ＿＿＿ ＿＿＿ ＿＿＿

e. D♭ major:　　　＿＿＿ ＿＿＿ ＿＿＿ ＿＿＿

f. A♭ major:　　　＿＿＿ ＿＿＿ ＿＿＿ ＿＿＿

g. C♯ minor: (natural)　＿＿＿ ＿＿＿ ＿＿＿ ＿＿＿

h. E♭ major:　　　＿＿＿ ＿＿＿ ＿＿＿ ＿＿＿

i. C minor (ascending melodic)　＿＿＿ ＿＿＿ ＿＿＿ ＿＿＿

j. A major:　　　＿＿＿ ＿＿＿ ＿＿＿ ＿＿＿

5. Name the modal degrees of the following scales.

a. G natural minor:　＿＿＿ ＿＿＿　　*d.* C♯ major:　＿＿＿ ＿＿＿

b. G♭ major:　　＿＿＿ ＿＿＿　　*e.* E major:　＿＿＿ ＿＿＿

c. B♭ major:　　＿＿＿ ＿＿＿　　*f.* F♯ natural minor:　＿＿＿ ＿＿＿

6. In the following melody, circle all the tonal degrees, cross out all the modal degrees, and place a small arrow pointing to each leading-tone.

Bach. *Two-Part Invention No. 1*

7. Circle all the tonal degrees of the following scales, and cross out all the modal degrees.

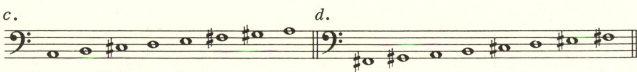

Dominant Harmony

8. Complete each of the following in four parts, note against note, according to the given tempos and rhythmic schemes. Use a variety of dynamics. When you have completed these, play each one several times.

Example

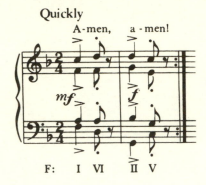

Quickly

A-men, a-men!

mf *f*

F: I   VI   II   V

a. Largo

G: I   VI   II   V

b. Moderato

d: I   VI   II   V

c. Fast and spirited

B♭:   I   VI   II   V

d. Moderato

e: I   VI   II   V

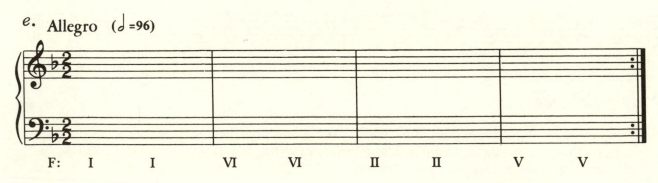

e. Allegro   (♩=96)

F: I   I   VI   VI   II   II   V   V

Tonal Strength of Chords

9. Name all keys (major and harmonic minor) that contain the following major chord:

 _____

10. Name all keys (major and harmonic minor) that contain both chords given below.

 _____

11. Name all major and harmonic minor keys containing the three chords below.

 _____

12. Name all major and harmonic minor keys having all four chords given below.

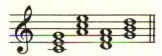 _____

Interchangeability of Modes

13. Work out a phrase in four parts in D major, note against note, according to the rhythm and harmony shown. Use root position only.

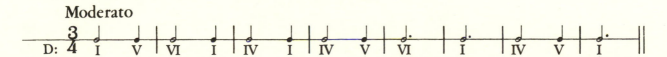

14. Renotate the phrase above in D harmonic minor.

15. Write a final version of the same phrase combining numbers 13 and 14. This version should be essentially major, enhanced by some minor color. For example, a Picardy 3rd at the end and/or a minor IV chord just before the end would achieve this purpose.

The Secondary Dominant Principle

16.

in C major is called V of _____.
in F major is called V of _____.
in B♭ major is called V of _____.

17.

in E♭ major is called V of _____.
in D minor is called V of _____.
in G minor is called V of _____.

18.

in C major is called V of _____.
in G minor is called V of _____.
in D minor is called V of _____.

SECTION C

Analysis

1. The following tunes are built upon modal scales. Name the keynote and write out the modal scale of each.

a.

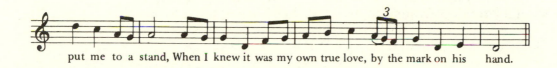

As I was a - walk-ing down in Stokes Bay, I___ met a drown-ed

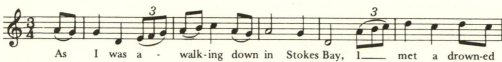

sail - or on___ the beach as he___ lay: And as I drew nigh him, it___

put me to a stand, When I knew it was my own true love, by the mark on his hand.

b.

Bach, Chorale No. 25, *Wo soll ich fliehen hin*

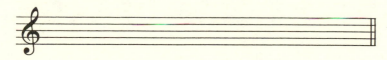

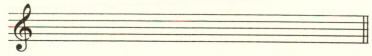

2. In the space provided below, write out the scale upon which each of the following pieces from the Anthology is based and name each mode.

a. 39b: Spatz (arr.), *Scarborough Fair*

b. 39a: Spatz (arr.), *The Second Farewell*

c. 39d: Spatz (arr.), *Motherless Children*

d. 7c: Jaffe (arr.), *Praise God from Whom All Blessings Flow* by Louis Bourgeois

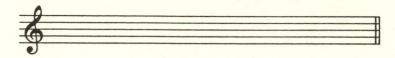

3. Analyze each of the following excerpts according to the procedure described on pages 19ff. Record the results of your analysis on the blank staves provided for that purpose.

a.

Clara Schumann, Impromptu *Le Sabbat*

b.

Duke Ellington, *Echoes of Harlem*

c.

Ich grol - le nicht   und wenn das Herz_____ auch bricht.

d.

Composition Activities

1. Write a melody for an unaccompanied wind instrument in E♭ major, $\frac{6}{8}$ or $\frac{3}{4}$ time, slow tempo. Limit the length of your melody to sixteen measures.

2. Write a folksong-like vocalise for medium-register unaccompanied voice on the syllable *la* or *oo*. Use the natural minor scale of C.

3. Write the first twelve measures of a meditative, basically homophonic piece in D major for piano and organ, suitable for a church service. Use one harmony per measure: I–IV–V–I–IV–I–V–VI–IV–II–V–I. Include some modal mixture.

4. Extend both melody and accompaniment of the following, using the harmony indicated.

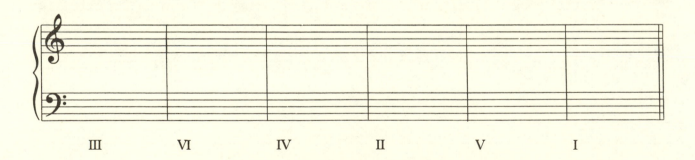

Self Test

1. The word _____ means "the organized relationship of pitches around a tonic" (see text, page 52).

2. _____ refers to the specific choice of the tones relating to a particular tonic.

3. Name the common modal scales, excluding major and natural

   minor: _____, _____, _____, and _____.

4. The Lydian scale _____ be constructed on the pitches G, B♭, C♯, or on any

   _{may/may not}

   of the other available pitches as tonal center.

5. The function of the _____ is to serve as the basis for the tonality of a composition.

6. _____ and _____ are the two scale degrees which "seem to give an impression of balanced support of the tonic, like two equidistant weights on either side of a fulcrum," (see text, page 54).

7. The tonal degrees of any major or minor scale are _____, _____, _____,

   and _____.

8. _____ and _____ are the modal degrees of A♭ major.

9. The modal degrees in any major or minor scale are _____ and _____.

10. The strongest harmonic element in tonal music is the _____ function.

11. The progressive V–I, found at the end of a phrase, is called the _____.

12. Elementary tonal units, that is, groups of two or three chords with distinct meaning as to key, may be referred to as _____.

13. A change of mode within a composition from major to minor, or vice versa, generally _____ affect the tonality.

    _{does/does not}

14. Interchange of modes is more probable when the prevailing mode is _____

    rather than _____.

15. When a composition with a prevailing minor mode ends on a major tonic triad, the

    effect is called _____.

16. When a tone other than the keynote of the prevailing key is made to be heard

    momentarily as tonic, the tone is said to be _____.

17. B major and B minor are said to be _____ modes.

18. Tones that are not members of the diatonic scale of the prevailing tonality are called

    _____ tones.

The First Inversion—The Figured Bass

SECTION A

Words and Ideas

Define in your own words

first inversion $\begin{smallmatrix}6\\3\end{smallmatrix}$ $\begin{smallmatrix}5\\3\end{smallmatrix}$ $\begin{smallmatrix}8\\5\\3\end{smallmatrix}$
7

2 $\begin{smallmatrix}6\\5\end{smallmatrix}$ $\begin{smallmatrix}4\\3\end{smallmatrix}$

figured bass   *fauxbourdon*   **VII**[6]

6♯, 6♭, 6♮   **6**   *basso continuo*

SECTION B

Exercises

Arabic-Numeral Notation

1. The following problems dealing with the realization of figured bass required two answers, in most cases:

   a. write in the pitch actually indicated by each figure; and
   b. write in the pitch or pitches not actually indicated by figures but implied by notational custom. (Doubling pitches need not be included.)

Example

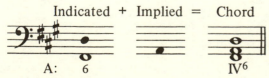

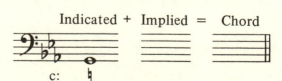

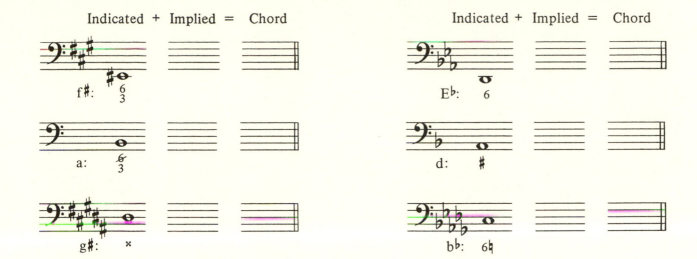

Indicated + Implied = Chord

Indicated + Implied = Chord

Doubling

2. Construct triads in four parts, according to the given pitches and figures. Use preferred doubling and spacing, and label each key and chord.

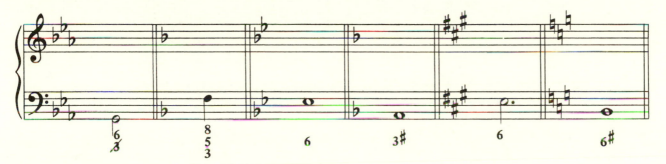

Voice Leading

3. Complete in four parts the progression I–V⁶–I in the keys indicated. Keep common tones in the same voice and move the other voices to their nearest available positions, with only the root being doubled.

4. Complete two four-part versions of each of the figured basses below. In the first version, common tones are to be kept in the same voice wherever possible, with minimal motion in the other parts; in the second version, the motion may be freer.

5. Realize the following figured basses in four parts, the upper parts moving freely. (In the second exercise below, the figures "7" indicate passing-tone sevenths on the second half of the beat; see the definition of passing tone in your text.)

c.

(after Beethoven)

SECTION C

Analysis

1. Analyze each of the following excerpts.

a.

Diabelli, *Sonata No. 4,* I

b.

Beethoven, *Variations on "Ich bin der Schneider Kakadu,"* op. 121a: Theme

(7)

c.

Mozart, *The Magic Flute*, Act I

Drei Knäb-chen, jung, schön, hold und wei - se, um-schwe - ben uns auf_ uns - rer_ Rei - se.

d.

Robert Johnson, *Com palefaced death*

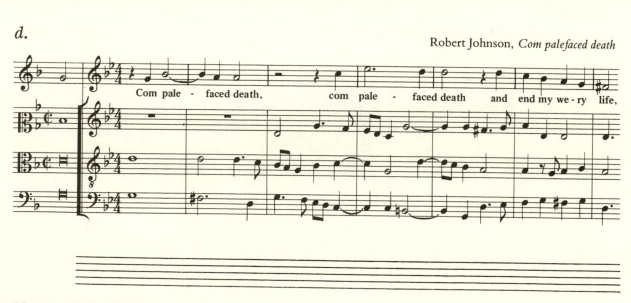

Com pale - faced death, com pale - faced death and end my we - ry life,

e.

2. Mark all first-inversion triads in each of the following Anthology pieces on the music itself.

   a. 43: Vivaldi, *The Seasons,* "Summer," entire movement

   b. 2: Bach, Prelude in C major from *The Well-Tempered Clavier,* mm. 1–9

   c. 4: Bach, *Sleepers, Awake,* entire chorale

   d. 11: Chopin, *Prelude,* Op. 28, No. 7, entire piece

SECTION D

Composition Activities

1. Extend the given measure in three different ways, according to the progressions indicated. Consider the left hand as accompaniment and the right hand as melody. Use a wide variety of note values in the melodic part.

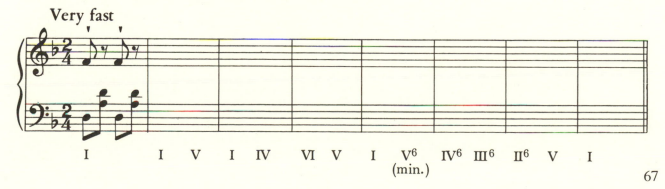

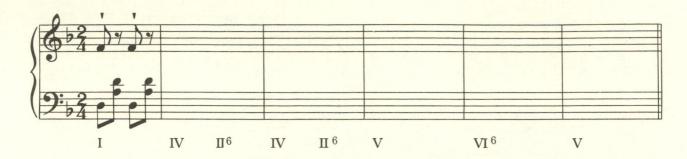

I   IV   II⁶   IV   II⁶   V   VI⁶   V

(Use chords of your own choice, but include at least two in the first inversion)

2. Write a keyboard piece based upon the succession of harmonies given below. You may use a freely variable texture of three to seven simultaneous parts, including doubling parts, in a chordal style appropriate to the piano, but written note against note. (The rests given apply to all parts at the moment they occur.)

(freely adapted from Schubert)

Andante moderato

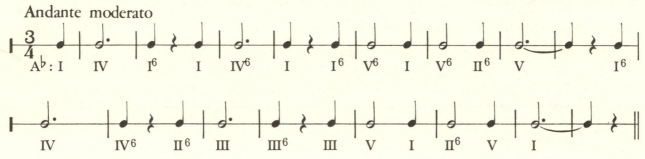

Self Test

1. In the first inversion of a triad, the _____ will be in the bass.

2. _____ is the arabic numeral that indicates that a triad is in the first inversion.

3. Roots are identified by _____ numerals, and inversions by _____ numerals.

4. The abbreviated form for indicating a tonic chord in the first inversion is _____.

5. $\frac{4}{3}$ is used to designate a seventh chord in _____ inversion.

6. A numeral ^{6} standing alone under a note in a figured bass provides what information, expressed or implied? _____

7. The choice of the tone for doubling in first-inversion chords is usually decided by what? _____

8. A chord labeled II$^6_4$ is said to be in the _____ inversion.

9. If a tonal degree is the bass note when a chord is in the first inversion, then this degree _____ usually doubled.
   is/is not

10. If the bass of a first-inversion triad is *not* a tonal degree, then usually it _____ doubled.
    is/is not

11. In a II^6 chord in G major, the preferred tone for doubling purposes is the _____

12. There _____ new principles of voice leading or of harmonic progression are several/are no
    involved in the use of triads in the first inversion.

13. The II^6 is very common at or near the end of a phrase in association with the _____ chord in cadences.

14. III^6 is not usually an independent chord; it is most often the result of a temporary displacement of tones of the _____ chord.

15. The augmented triad in the minor mode appears _____ in first inversion.
    most often/never

16. IV^6 is a useful alternative to _____ when following V, when stepwise motion in the bass is desired.

17. The third of the dominant triad is the _____ of the key.

18. VI^6 often stands in place of the _____ chord.

19. In VII^6 the preferred doubling is of _____, though the _____ may also be doubled; on the other hand, the _____ is seldom doubled.

20. The method of denoting upper voices above a given bass note, using arabic numeration, is called _____.

21. A line drawn vertically or slantwise through an arabic numeral in a figured bass will indicate _____

22. An accidental in isolation below the bass note, not attached to any arabic numeral, always indicates _____

23. A horizontal line following a numeral signifies _____

Function and Structure of Melody

SECTION A

Words and Ideas

Define and memorize:

melody	**theme**	**countermelody**
obbligato	**descant**	**collateral part**
cantus firmus	**chorales**	**tune**
symphonic melody	**development**	**ostinato**
ground bass	**roulade**	**figuration**
melodic contour	**anacrusis**	**motive**
phrase	**cadence**	**antecedent**
consequent	**analytical reduction**	**compound line**
variation	**ornamentation, ornament**	**arpeggiation**

SECTION B

Exercises

Reduction Techniques

1. Make an analytical reduction of the following fragments by removing repeated successions of triadic factors and notating them as a single simultaneous chord.

a.

Corelli, *Sonata I* for Violin and Continuo, Op, V, No. 1

b. **Allegro** (♩ = 112)
largamente

2. The melodies given below suggest compound lines. Provide melodic reductions which will show one way of hearing the two lines separately.

a.

Loewe, *Der Feind*

Der Ad - ler lauscht auf sei - nem Horst; der Kei - ler rauscht zur Kes - sel-forst; das Kätz - lein klingt am Ast sich fest;

b.

Vivaldi, *Sonata* for Cello and Continuo, Allegro

71

3. Complete a reduction for each of the following melodic lines, according to the procedure demonstrated in the text. (See Examples 7–27 and 7–28, and accompanying text.)

a.

Haydn, *Symphony No. 100* ("Military"), III

b.

Smetana, *The Moldau*

c.

Tchaikovsky, *Capriccio Italien*

Analysis

1. On the next page is a four-measure excerpt from Beethoven's *Ninth Symphony*, show-
ing a rich texture of different melodic types distributed among a chorus and the
instruments of a large orchestra. Find within the excerpt the following melodic types
and list them by indicating the parts in which they occur and their measure numbers:

   a. The "tune" which is the principal melody. (Include duplicating parts.) _____

   _____

   b. Parts that form a chordal texture with the principal melody but that do not have

      any particular prominence. _____

   c. An "interior accompaniment." _____

   d. A countermelody. _____

   e. A collateral part. _____

   f. A significant repeated-note figure. _____

   g. Figurational activity. _____

2. Identify each of the melody types in the excerpts below. Write your answers on the
score.

   a.

Bruckner, Te Deum: "Aeterna fac cum Sanctis"

(cont. on p. 75)

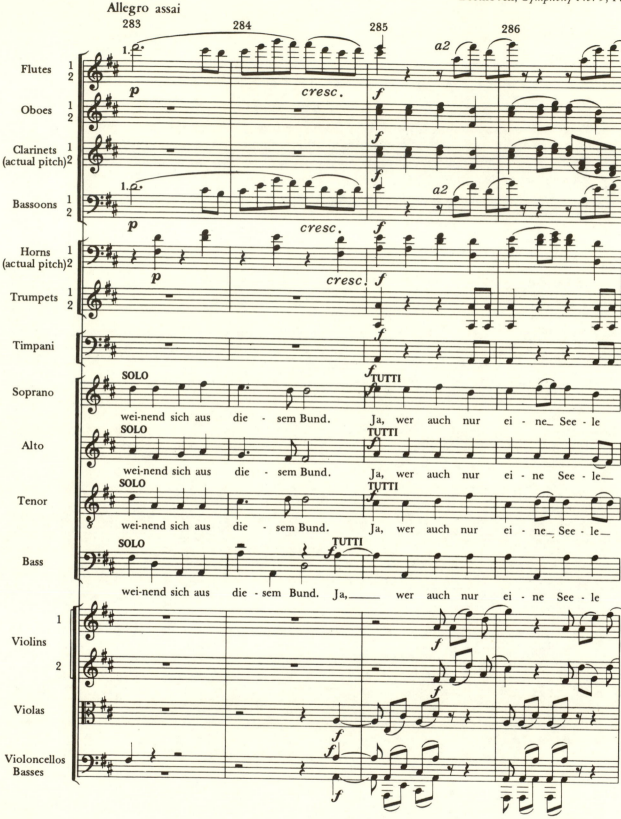

(cont. from p. 73)

b.

Brahms, *Intermezzo in C*, Op. 119, No. 3

Grazioso e giocoso

molto **p** e legg.

3. Identify each of the melody types in the following excerpts from the Anthology. Write your answers on the music.

a. 4: Bach, Chorale: *Sleepers, Awake*

b. 36: Saint-Saens, *The Carnival of the Animals,* "The Elephant"

c. 33: Mussorgsky, Coronation Scene (excerpt) from *Boris Godunov,* Prologue, Scene II

Composition Activities

Note: From here on, you will provide your own manuscript paper for all composition activities.

1. Write an eight-measure melody for violin in D minor that could be used as a theme for a symphony movement.

2. Transpose the melody above to G minor and write a countermelody for a second violin.

3. Rewrite your theme in A minor and add a part for viola.

4. Write a dance tune for piano, eight measures long, with an ostinato as accompaniment.

5. Write a figurational melody that could be used to accompany either the theme or the tune that you have written as part of the activities above.

6. Write a three-note melodic idea that is special in terms of its pitch and rhythmic organization. Use this as a motive in an original melody of two four-measure phrases. Write this for an instrument of your choice.

7. Write a pair of matched phrases in antecedent and consequent relationship for an instrument of your choice.

8. Write five melodic variations on the tune that you wrote for number 4 above.

9. Write five melodic variations on the theme that you wrote for number 1 above.

Self Test

1. The word _____ describes any group of tones meant to be heard as a succession.

2. A succession of tones, nearly as interesting as, but deliberately contrasted with, a principal melody, both rhythmically and contrapuntally, is called a _____ _____.

3. A countermelody for solo instrument in combination with a solo singer and additional harmonic accompaniment is called an _____.

4. A descant is _____ _____.

5. A collateral part parallels, or follows the line of, a principal melody, most usually in intervals of _____ or _____.

6. A theme generally associated with sacred music consisting of regularly spaced notes, usually surrounded by a faster moving texture is called a _____ _____.

7. The principal melody of a song or a dance is usually referred to as a _____.

8. The process of change involving the melodic idea of a composition is called _____.

9. A short melody, usually in the bass, that repeats over and over again is called _____.

10. A succession of tones in a repeated pattern that projects harmony more than melody is called a _____.

11. A _____ is a short thematic unit, melodic or rhythmic or both, which is subject to repetition and transformation.

12. Another name for "upbeat" is _____.

13. A perceived unit of musical thought which measures the beginning and ending of a melodic unit is called a _____.

14. The end of a phrase is called the _____.

15. The terms _____ and _____ indicate phrases in natural pairs, in which the second phrase seems to complement or answer the first.

16. _____ is the adding of decorative tones to a subsequent appearance of a melodic unit in such a way that its original form or profile can still be discerned.

Nonharmonic Tones

SECTION A

Words and Ideas

Define in your own words:

melodic dissonance	nonharmonic tones	passing tone (p.t., P)
neighbor note (N)	auxiliary tone (aux.)	double neighbor tone
neighbor chord	incomplete neighbor (IN)	anticipation (ant.)
appoggiatura (app.)	appoggiatura chord	suspension (S)
escape tone (E)	reaching tone (R)	échappée
cambiata	ornamental resolution	free tone
pedal, pedal point		

SECTION B

Exercises

1. Work out two versions of the figured bass line below. Have all nonharmonic tones move in eighth notes, except in the last measure, where they may move in quarters.

First Version: Include a number of passing and neighbor tones.

(adapted from Schumann)

Second Version: Incorporate a number of anticipations and appoggiatura.

2. Work out two versions of the figured bass line below, as follows:

First Version: Incorporate suspensions and escape tones.

Second Version: Include reaching tones and at least one pedal tone.

3. Realize the following figured bass in four parts, the upper parts moving mostly in eighth and sixteenth notes, freely incorporating nonharmonic tones of *all* types. Include at least two instances of successive nonharmonic tones (see text, especially Examples 8–38, 39, and 40). A rest in the bass does not necessarily call for rests in the upper parts.

SECTION C

Analysis

1. The following two-voice fragments contain various types of nonharmonic tones. Determine their type and precise location, indicating each with the appropriate symbol or abbreviation (P, N, S, etc.). In some instances the complete chord is not present, but the roman numeral below each example will guide you.

F: VI   IV   C: V   A: VI   V   a: V   II^6 B♭: V^6 VI^6

c: VI   I   G: I   V$^6_4$ C: V_____   A: V_____

A: II^6 V   d: I_____   C: V_____   F: I_____

F: I   II   I   E♭: I   II^6 C: IV_____   A: V^7_____

2. For each of the following excerpts, complete a key–chord analysis and record your results on the blank staves that are provided. When you have identified each chord, circle those tones that are melodic dissonances, or nonharmonic tones, and label each type (P, N, S, etc.).

a.

Bach, Prelude No. 4 from *The Well-Tempered Clavier*

Andante con moto. ($\quad$ = 92)

p sempre legato.

cresc.

Schumann, *Trio*, Op. 110, IV

Kräftig, mit Humor. (♩ = 104.)

c.

Mason, *Dance Antique*, Op. 38

Allegro

d.

Allegretto

e.   Schumann, *The Little Morning Wanderer,* No. 17 from *Album for the Young,* Op. 68

Schwächer

3. The following pieces from the Anthology provide excellent study in the use of melodic dissonance, or nonharmonic tones. On the score, complete a key–chord analysis; also circle and label all nonharmonic tones.

a. 3: Bach, *Toccata in D minor,* mm. 1–16.

b. 6: Beethoven, *Sonata in A♭,* Op. 26, I, theme.

c. 15b: L. Couperin, *Double on Rigaudon,* entire piece.

d. 17: Dandrieu, *Magnificat,* entire piece.

Composition Activities

1. An accompaniment is given below. Write a melody to go with it, using chord tones and passing tones only. Write a second version using suspensions with ornamental resolutions, plus passing tones and neighbor notes, as you wish. A third version should use all nonharmonic tone types.

(adapted from Schumann)

2. The melodies given below are actually the basic pitches of well-known tunes. It may be that as you perform these activities you will guess the names of the tunes. More important, however, is for you to work out four variations of each of these tunes as follows:

First variation: Use chord tones freely and use those passing tones and neighbor notes that seem musically appropriate.

Second variation: Free use of chord tones as well as reaching tones and escape tones.

Third variation: Free use of chord tones as well as anticipations and suspensions.

Fourth variation: Free use of chord tones and any of the above nonharmonic tones, as you wish. Required use of appoggiaturas.

a. Slowly

b. Moderately

Note: You have no choice but to use a suspension in the middle of m. 7 in all variations. The chord on the second half of m. 11 is a secondary dominant: G–B♮–D–F.

Self Test

1. The term *melodic dissonance* describes dissonance in a musical texture resulting from the inclusion of _____ tones.

2. Do nonharmonic tones, nonchord tones, and nontriadic tones all represent essentially the same phenomenon? _____

3. A minimum of two voices sounding simultaneously is needed to produce melodic dissonance: true or false? _____

4. Our recognition of nonharmonic tones suggests that dissonance in tonal music is rigidly controlled, and that in this control _____ motion plays an important
   conjunct/disjunct
   part.

5. Any dissonance in tonal music must have a possible stepwise resolution to a _____ .

6. Melodic motion can both generate and _____ dissonance.

7. The neighbor note (auxiliary) and the passing tone involve only _____ motion.

8. The motion to and from a neighbor note is always stepwise and in the _____ direction.

9. The neighbor note is always a _____ beat or part of the beat.

10. A tone that in all respects is like a neighbor note, but that falls on a strong beat, is called _____ .

11. The _____ consists of the advance sounding of a tone as a sort of upbeat.

12. The nonharmonic tone that fills a melodic skip by means of stepwise motion in the same direction is called a _____ .

13. Passing tones are always _____ . Otherwise, they would be called appoggiature.

14. What is a suspension? _____

15. A suspended tone that is not tied, but is reattacked on the strong beat, is called an _____ , though it is a particular type in that it is prepared.

16. The nonharmonic tone usually involving a step–skip motion and which is usually metrically weak is called _____ .

17. A leap up or down, followed by stepwise motion in the opposite direction is called _____ .

18. *Échappée* and *cambiata* are older names for _____ and _____ respectively.

UNIT NINE
Harmonization of a Melody

There is no section A for this unit.

SECTION B

Exercises

Available Chords

1. Below is a three-note fragment in F major. Using diatonic triads only, determine which three chords would work as supporting harmony for each given pitch. List the available chords by letter names of roman numerals below each pitch.

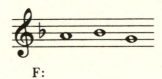

F:

2. Harmonize the same fragment using two- or three-chord progressions appropriate for the beginning of a melody in F major. Good four-part writing is, of course, expected.

F:

86

Analysis of the Melody

3. The melodic fragment below may be interpreted in at least four different keys. Consider these pitches as ending a melodic phrase. Select chords that will strengthen the tonality and at the same time provide the harmonic formula for a half or an authentic cadence, as appropriate. Work these out in four parts.

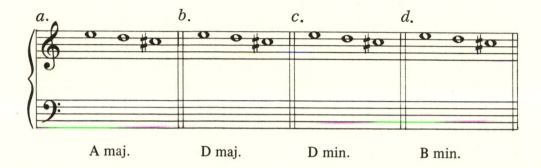

A maj.   D maj.   D min.   B min.

4. Consider that each of the following should end on a half cadence in G. The first two pitches may be harmonized with one or two chords. Each should be somewhat different from the other, and correctly worked out in four parts.

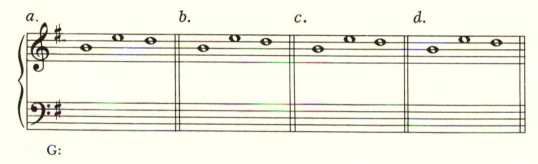

G:

5. The three pitches below should be considered as part of a phrase. Provide two consecutive chords for one of the pitches in each of your four-part harmonizations.

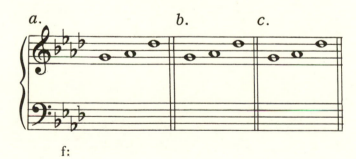

f:

6. The first two pitches are to be interpreted as belonging to the same harmony. Create three different harmonizations of this fragment, demonstrating correct four-part writing.

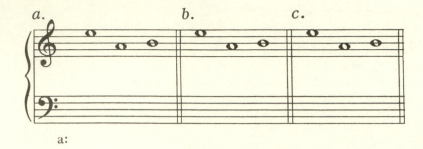

a:

Selection of Chords and Contrapuntal Approach: Melody and Bass

7. The following three-note soprano fragment is given with several alternative basses. You are to supply the missing note in each bass. In all of these exercises *always* select chords that will reflect "most usual" progressions from the "Table of Root Progressions" (see Chapter 3). All of the chords do not have to be in root position as you complete these exercises demonstrating correct four-part writing.

a.

D:

b.

c#:

c.

Bb:

8. Consider the melody below as a single phrase with an internal extension and an authentic cadence. In this exercise, all pitches will be considered as chord tones.
Your harmonization will have to take into account the following:

a. the tonality and modality

b. the cadences

c. the harmonic rhythm:

      (1) when melodic skips suggest the same chord

      (2) when sustained pitches will be harmonized by one or more chords

d. an inventory of all possible chords

e. strength of tonality balanced with the need for variety

f. a bass line that enhances and complements the soprano line

Keeping all of the above in mind, work out three versions of this Schubert melody in four parts.

Schubert, *To Sylvia* (text originally from Shakespeare, *The Two Gentlemen of Verona*)

Who is Sil-via? What is she,— that all our swains com-mend her?

a.

b.

c.

9. Work out a fourth version of the Schubert melody, allowing some of the melodic pitches to function as nonharmonic tones. This will give you much more freedom and variety in your choice of harmonic rhythm.

10. Harmonize the following phrases drawn from chorale melodies. You may consider any appropriate pitch a nonharmonic tone.

a.

Jesu Leiden, Pein und Tod

b.

Schwing' dich auf zu deinem Gott

c.

Allein Gott in der Höh' sei Ehr

d.

Nun sich der Tag geendet hat

e.

Gott der Vater, wohn' uns bei

f.

Herr, ich habe missgehandelt

Analysis

1. Examine the first two phrases of each of the following Anthology pieces. (Show ends of phrases with a bracket, ⌐———⌐, placed just above the music.) Provide at least one reharmonization of each two-phrase melody, giving consideration to:
   a. keeping the melody as is but harmonizing it in a key that is different from the original;
   b. harmonizing with fewer chords;
   c. harmonizing with a greater number of chords.

   a. 7a: Louis Bourgeois, *Praise God from Whom All Blessings Flow*

   b. 19: Stephen Foster, *Beautiful Dreamer* (omit introduction)

   c. 22: Edvard Grieg, "The Death of Ase" from *Peer Gynt Suite No. 1*

SECTION D

Composition Activities

1*a.* Provide a realization of the melody below, using the chords indicated. Make sure your four-part writing is correct.
  b. Provide an alternate realization, adding in or substituting chords that you feel would be musically appropriate.

2. Provide two realizations for the melody below, following the same instructions as those of question 1 above.

3. Provide an alternate harmonization for the following tunes in the Anthology:

    a. 39b: *Scarborough Fair*

    b. 39c: *The Irish Washerwoman*

    c. 39f: *Off to California*

SECTION E

Self Test

1. When a melody moves by skip it is often advisable to use _____ harmony for both notes.
(the same/different)

2. Against a single sustained melodic tone there _____ be chord changes occurring during its total length.
(may/may not)

3. Considering triads only, each given tone of the melody has _____ possible diatonic chords available for harmonization.

4. The Tables of Usual Root Progressions in Chapters 3 and 4 _____ helpful in determining the possible choices of chords in the harmonization of a melody.
(are/are not)

5. The use of chords in first inversion _____ useful in providing further possibilities for shaping the bass melody.
(is/is not)

6. When using root position and first inversion triads there are _____ intervals possible between the soprano and the bass.

7. A vocabulary of "harmonic words" _____ extremely useful in planning a harmonization.
(is/is not)

The Six-Four Chord

Words and Ideas

Define in your own words:

six-four chord   **cadential six-four chord**   **auxiliary six-four chord**
passing six-four chord   **arpeggiating six-four chord**

Exercises

The Cadential Six-Four Chord

1. Work out each of the following in four parts, note against note, and in a variety of chord spacings. Label all chords with appropriate roman and arabic numerals. (Your solution to these will provide a good reference source for the six-four chord as it is usually employed.)

94

The Auxiliary Six-Four Chord

2. Work out the following as specified for the cadential six-four chord, above.

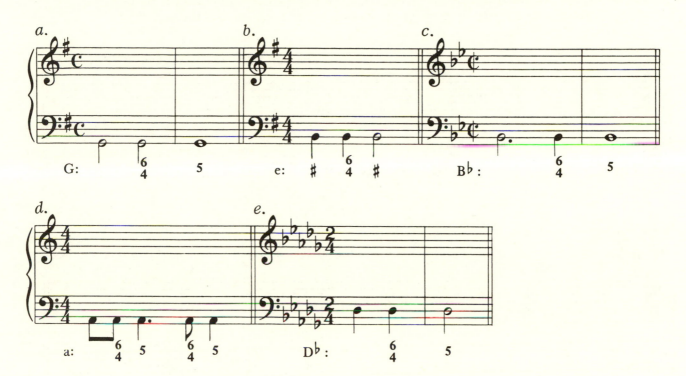

The Passing Six-Four Chord

3. Work out the following as specified for the cadential six-four chord, above.

Supplementary Exercises

4. Various uses of the six-four chord are represented in the following figured bases derived from the literature. As you work these out in four parts, indicate the function of each six-four chord by writing "cadential," "passing," etc., as the case may be.

a.

Schubert, *Valses sentimentales,* Op. 50 (freely adapted)

b. **Presto**

Beethoven, *Trio,* Op. 97 ("Archduke"), IV (freely adapted)

c.

Schubert, *Graz Waltzes,* Op. 91a (adapted)

d. **Allegro**

Mozart, *Rondo,* K. 485 (adapted)

Analysis

1. Examine each of the following excerpts. Complete a key-chord analysis on the staff provided. Determine whether or not each excerpt is a complete phrase. Use brackets (└──────┘) beneath the roman numerals to highlight those chords involved in the particular six-four chord use. Label each use beneath this bracket (cadential, passing, etc.).

a.   Clementi, *Sonatina*, Op. 36, No. 4, III

b.   Mozart, *Violin Sonata*, K. 301, I

Allegro con spirito

c.   Beethoven, *Piano Concerto No. 1,* Op. 15, I

Allegro con brio

d.

e.

J. C. Bach, *Duet No. 3* from *Six Duets*

2. For additional review, choose eight-measure excerpts from three different Anthology pieces and complete the procedure you followed in question 1 above.

Composition Activities

1. Return to the realizations you wrote for questions 1 and 2 on page 92. Integrate six-four chords into your realizations of 1a and 2a.
2. Add or substitute appropriate six-four chords to the following pieces from the Anthology. Indicate on the score where these additions or substitutions could occur.

   a. 39b: *Scarborough Fair*

   b. 39c: *The Irish Washerwoman*

   c. 39f: *Off to California*

SECTION E

Self Test

1. When a triad is in the _____ inversion it is called a six-four chord.
2. The _____ of the chord is in the bass when the triad is in the six-four position.
3. The dissonant interval that exists when a major or minor triad is in the six-four position is the _____.
4. The six-four chord is thought of generally as _____ chord.
   a stable/an unstable
5. The chord factor that is most usually doubled in the six-four chord is the _____.
6. A strong tonic six-four, usually unprepared, and resolving to a dominant chord as a double appoggiatura, is called a _____ six-four.
7. The distinguishing characteristics of the cadential six-four are:

   a. _____ b. _____ and

   c. _____

8. The motion of the voices in the resolution of the cadential tonic six-four to the dominant is _____ by _____.
9. The cadential six-four _____ often placed immediately after the barline.
   is/is not

10. The six-four in which two factors function as neighbor notes is the _____ six-four chord.

11. The auxiliary six-four chord is usually on a _____ beat.

12. The distinguishing characteristics of the auxiliary six-four are:

    a. _____ b. _____ and

    c. _____.

13. The passing six-four chord gets its name from the motion of the _____.

14. A typical chord progression involving the passing six-four chord could be: _____
_____   _____

_____

15. The distinguishing characteristics of the passing six-four are:

    a. _____ b. _____ and

    c. _____

16. Triads built on the _____ degrees of the scale are more often found in the

    six-four position than are those built on _____ degrees.

Cadences

SECTION A

Words and Ideas

Define in your own words:

cadence   **authentic cadence**   **perfect authentic cadence**
half cadence   **semicadence**   **downbeat cadence**
upbeat cadence   **deceptive cadence**   **Phrygian cadence**
exceptional cadences

SECTION B

Exercises

The Authentic Cadence

1. Work out the following exercise in four parts. Label all cadences as well as all chords and inversions. Identify all six-four chord usages by type.

Andantino

Mozart, *The Magic Flute*, Act I (adapted)

2. Work out two different approaches to the authentic cadence above. You may change the bass pitches and chords of the last two measures as seems appropriate. Play and compare these with the original above.

Perfect Cadences

3. Are the cadences in the exercises above perfect? Below, provide alternate versions of these cadences so that in the end you will have at least one cadence that is perfect and one that is not.

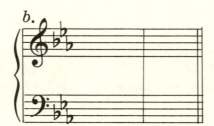

Half Cadence

4. The following calls for a half cadence at measure four, and ends with an extended authentic cadence. Work it out in four parts and label all chords, cadences, and inversions. Compare the effects of the two cadences.

Haydn, *Sonata No. 3,* I (adapted)

Presto

5. Work out in four parts and provide all necessary labels.

Beethoven, *Sonata,* Op. 31, No. 2 ("Tempest"), I

6. Work out in four parts and label.

Mozart, *Sonata,* K. 576, I (adapted)

7. Disregard the figures and bass notes of the last two measures in exercise 6 above and work out two alternate endings involving half cadences. Compare with the original.

a.   *b.*

Plagal Cadence

8. Work out in four parts and label.

Handel, *Messiah*, Hallelujah Chorus (adapted)

Allegro

9. Work out substitute plagal cadences for Exercise 8 above.

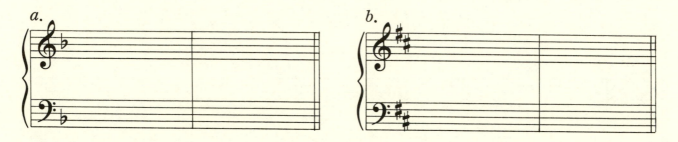

Downbeat and Upbeat Cadences

10. This concept, though simple, is nevertheless very important. Play through any of the exercises above, as well as those that follow, altering the duration of the last few chords to produce upbeat and downbeat cadential effects. Notate the duration values above the staff that would change the effect of the cadence for all the exercises in this section.

The Deceptive Cadence

11. Supply alternative endings that produce a deceptive cadential effect for Exercise 1 on page 101 and the first half of 4 on page 102. Create two versions of each, the first an upbeat cadence and the second a downbeat cadence.

12. Supply an alternate ending for Exercise 1 on page 101 that has a Phrygian cadential effect.

SECTION C

Analysis

1. Above the symbol used to indicate the end of a phrase (⌐‾‾‾‾‾‾⌐), which you are to draw on the examples below, indicate the cadence type, using the following abbreviations:

     AC = Authentic Cadence
    PAC = Perfect Authentic Cadence
     HC = Half Cadence
     DC = Deceptive Cadence
     PC = Plagal Cadence
    PhC = Phrygian Cadence

a.

Christus, der ist mein Leben (Melody: Melchior Vulpius)

b.

c.

Loewe, *Die Oasis* from *Arabischer Liederkreis*

106

2. Locate and identify all cadences in the following Anthology pieces, giving appropriate measure numbers.

a. 23: Handel, *Joy to the World*

_____

_____

_____

_____

b. 25: Haydn, *Der Greis*

_____

_____

_____

_____

c. 31: Mozart, Sonata in A Major, K. 331, I Theme

_____

_____

_____

_____

SECTION D

Composition Activities

1. Return to the realization you wrote for Exercise 1 on page 92. Substitute a different cadence for each interior cadence in your realization. In order to do this, you will have to alter at least one harmony, and perhaps two or more. It may also be necessary to change some of the pitches of the melody.

When this is completed, compare each phrase with the original in terms of the degree of finality projected. Also consider the effect of the whole with its substituted cadences.

2. Complete the same process for the realization of Exercise 2 on page 92.

3. Create six different endings for the following phrase by adding:
   a. an authentic cadence
   b. a perfect authentic cadence
   c. a plagal cadence
   d. a deceptive cadence
   e. a half cadence
   f. a plagal cadence following an authentic cadence

Self Test

1. Harmonic formulae used for phrase endings which "mark the breathing places in music, establish or confirm the tonality, and render coherent the formal structure" are called _____.

2. The authentic cadence comprises at least the progression _____ to _____.

3. The chord commonly preceding the authentic cadential formula will often be either ____ or _____.

4. The authentic cadential formula _____ be preceded by I_4^6.

may/may not

5. The progression IV–I_4^6–V–I appearing at a final cadence will be very _____ strong/weak in terms of its finality.

6. The most conclusive arrangement of the authentic cadence, with tonic and dominant chords in root position and the tonic note in the soprano at the end, is called a _____ authentic cadence.

7. An authentic cadence that is not perfect is considered to be _____ final.

more/less

8. When the final chord of a cadential harmonic formula is a dominant, then the cadence is called a _____ cadence.

9. The plagal cadence "is most often used after an authentic cadence, as sort of added close to a movement," and consists of the harmonic progression _____ to _____.

10. The minor form of subdominant harmony _____ used in the plagal cadence

is occasionally/is never
    at the end of a movement in the major mode.

11. The _____ cadence "is similar to the authentic except that some other chord is substituted for the final tonic."

12. The chord most frequently substituted for the tonic in the deceptive cadence is the _____ chord.

13. A IV^6–V final cadence in the minor mode, appearing at the end of a slow movement or slow introduction, is called a _____ cadence.

UNIT TWELVE
Harmonic Rhythm

Words and Ideas

Define in your own words:

meter   **rhythm**   **agogic stress**
pulse   **melodic rhythm**   **rhythmic texture**
static harmony **harmonic rhythm**   **nonharmonic chords**

SECTION B

Exercises

1. Derive the melodic rhythm from each of the following excerpts, using Examples 12–1 and 12–2 in the text as your model.

a.

Schaut, ihr Sünder (Melody: M. A. von Löwenstern)

1.

2.

3.

4.

b.

c.

Harmonic Rhythm and Melodic Rhythm

2. Return to the exercises above and derive the harmonic rhythm in the manner demonstrated in Example 12–3 of the text. Notate your answers above each exercise.

Frequency of Root Change

3. Return to Exercise 1 again and examine each excerpt for the frequency of root change. Would you describe it as regular or irregular? Is it static, active, or neither of these? Place your answers below.

a. _____   _____

b. _____   _____

c. _____   _____

Strength of Harmonic Progression

4. Based on your observations of examples 1a–1c, what is your assessment of the strength of the harmonic progressions in each excerpt? Is it best described as strong, weak, or a mixture of strong and weak? Place your answers below.

a. _____

b. _____

c. _____

Supplementary Exercises

5. Realize the derived figured bases given below and notate harmonic rhythm above each example.

a.   Mozart, *Piano Concerto*, K. 456, I (adapted)

b.

Allegro

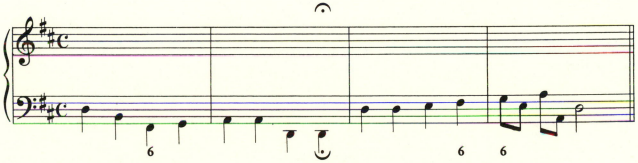

c.

Bach, Chorale No. 153, *Alle Menschen müssen sterben*

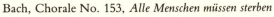

6. Realize the following unfigured basses in four parts, using root–position and inverted chords.

   a. Provide a relatively static harmonic rhythm, using primarily strong progressions.

Wagner, *Lohengrin,* Act II,, scene 4: Elsa's Procession

b. Provide a moderately active harmonic rhythm, with a good mixture of strong and weak progressions.

Chopin, *Mazurka,* Op. 68, No. 3 (adapted)

Allegro ma non troppo

SECTION C

Analysis

1. Complete a key–chord analysis of the following excerpts, notating harmonic rhythm above the staff.

a.

Beethoven, *Sonata,* Op. 10, No. 1, II

Adagio molto

b.

c.

Brahms, *Rhapsody,* Op. 79, No. 2

2. Compare the harmonic rhythm of the following pairs of pieces from the Anthology and briefly describe your findings.

   a. *32: Mozart, Sonata in D Major, K. 284, I, Theme*
       34: Old Welsh Air, *Deck the Halls*

   b. 35: Purcell, Prelude from Suite No. 1 in G Major
               Almand from Suite No. 1 in G Major

   c. 36: Saint-Saëns, The Elephant from *The Carnival of the Animals*
       43: Vivaldi, "Summer," II from *The Seasons*

Composition Activities

1. Compose an original melody consisting of two phrases (a minimum of four measures each). Provide chord symbols above this melody (lead-sheet fashion) suggesting three different harmonizations in accordance with the following:
   a. an extremely static harmonic rhythm
   b. an extremely active harmonic rhythm
   c. an harmonic rhythm that is neither of the above

2. Realize, in four parts, two versions of each of the above, demonstrating for each:
   a. melodic rhythm that is more active than the harmonic rhythm.
   b. melodic rhythm that is *as active* as the harmonic rhythm.

Self Test

1. Frequency of _____ change and the _____ quality of the change are the two main features of harmonic rhythm.

2. Is the harmonic rhythm affected when a chord merely changes position, whether or not the bass is repeated? _____

3. Any assessment of the harmonic rhythm of a composition _____ include a
   consideration of the dynamics of the music. _{should/need not}

4. Some chords that primarily for rhythmic reasons do not attain the status of independent harmonies are called _____ chords.

5. Harmonic rhythm _____ correspond to the meter.
   must always/need not

6. In common time, when a chord is introduced on the first or third beat it is said to have relative _____ .

7. When the harmonic changes are few and far between, the harmonic rhythm is said to be _____ .

8. Very frequent changes of harmony create a feeling of _____ .

9. The presence of a pedal point tends to create a _____ harmonic layer in the music, which may otherwise be active.

Harmonic Structure of the Phrase

SECTION A

Words and Ideas

Define in your own words:

unity and variety	**thesis**	**anacrusis**
connective melody	**overlapping voices**	**harmonic sequence**
regular sequence	**half sequence**	**antecedent**
consequent	**period**	**closed forms**
binary	**ternary**	*da capo* **form**
open forms		

SECTION B

Exercises

Note: From this point on, in all exercises in realization of a figured bass or harmonization of an unfigured bass, you should assume that free motion of the upper parts is permitted unless otherwise indicated; in other words, the note-against-note restriction no longer holds automatically. "Free motion" will of course include the use of nonharmonic tones, whether or not they are indicated.

Unity and Variety

1. Work out the following *unfigured bass* in four parts (SATB). Label key(s), chords, and inversions. In the selection and distribution of chords attempt to achieve a maximum of unity and a minimum of variety.

2. With regard to 1 immediately above, briefly explain how you achieved unity through:

a. Chord selection: _____

_____

b. Chord distribution: _____

_____

3. As you work out the following unfigured bass in four parts, attempt to provide for a maximum of variety through chord selection and distribution, while providing only a minimum of unity in terms of tonal strength.

4. Briefly explain how you achieved a maximum of variety through chord selection and distribution while maintaining a minimum of unity in question 3, immediately above.

_____

_____

_____

5. Work out the following figured bass in four parts. Label key(s), chords, and inversions.

(adapted from Bach, *The Well-Tempered Clavier,* Book II: Prelude No. 19)

6. In question 5, immediately above, how has Bach achieved unity through chord selection?

_____

7. In reference to 5 above, comment briefly upon the variety provided by the distribution of chords.

_____

Number of Measures in the Phrase

8. Examine selection 9 from the Anthology, _America_, and answer the following:

a.

	Number of measures	Number of chord changes
First phrase	_____	_____
Second phrase	_____	_____
Third phrase	_____	_____

b. Has phrase extension of any type been used in any of the phrases? _____ If yes, what type? _____

The Phrase Beginning

c. In _America_ observe the beginning of each phrase and then fill in the following blanks.

	Choice of first chord	Anacrusis or thesis
First phrase	_____	_____
Second phrase	_____	_____
Third phrase	_____	_____

Connection of Phrases

d. Are the successive phrases in _America_ connected by (1) melodic linkage, (2) bass motion, (3) overlapping of phrases, or (4) none of the above?

First–second phrase _____

Second–third phrase _____

e. Does harmonic sequence play a part in the organization of the piece? _____ If yes, explain. _____

f. Do any adjacent phrase pairs constitute a period?

	yes / no
First–second phrase	_____
Second–third phrase	_____

SECTION C

Analysis

Below are some guidelines for analysis of the harmonic structure of a phrase, given in the form of questions to be answered. The guidelines are intended first to assist you in the exercises that follow, but you should also refer to them, if you need to, when analyzing any music from this viewpoint.

Guidelines for Analysis of the Harmonic Structure of a Phrase

1. What is the average number of measures included in the phrase?
2. What is the average number of harmonies per phrase?
3. Are tonal-degree triads used principally?
4. Are modal-degree triads used at all?
5. Are first-inversion triads used only occasionally, moderately, or quite frequently?
6. What chord is used to begin each phrase?
7. What is the chord used at the cadence?
8. Is the end of the phrase upbeat or downbeat?
9. Is the melodic rhythm the same, somewhat different, or quite different from the harmonic rhythm?
10. Does the harmonic rhythm coincide with the meter?
11. Which adjacent phrase pairs form periods?
12. Is any given phrase a literal, or almost literal repeat of any other phrase in the composition?

Apply the guidelines above to each of the three pieces from the Anthology listed below. Record your answers in the blank spaces.

Guideline	37: Schumann	38: Sousa	1a: J. C. Bach
1			
2			
3			
4			
5			
6			
7			
8			
9			
10			
11			
12			

Composition Activities

1. Write a pair of phrases that form a period.
2. Rewrite the period, extending each phrase by one or two measures by:
   First phrase: extending an idea within the phrase.
   Second phrase: repeating exactly part of the ending of the second phrase, to include at least the cadential formula.
3. Now write three additional versions of the periods in questions 1, and 2, immediately above, as follows:
   First version: melodically link each phrase pair.
   Second version: link each phrase pair by bass motion.
   Third version: allow the last chord of the first phrase to function also as the first chord of the second phrase.

Self Test

1. The number of measures in a phrase will usually be _____.

2. In most phrases there will probably be _____ changes of harmony than there are beats in the phrase.
   more/fewer

3. Eight measures, in a moderate tempo, very probably will constitute a relatively

   _____ phrase.
   long/short

4. *Thesis* is another word for _____, while *anacrusis* refers to

   the _____.

5. The _____ always signals the phrase ending, just as the beginning of a

   phrase can be determined by locating the _____ of the previous phrase.

6. Cadential types have been compared to punctuation marks, with

   the _____ cadence being in effect like the comma, and the _____
   cadence being comparable to the full stop, or period.

7. If the final chord is on a strong beat the ending is called a _____; otherwise

   it is called an _____ ending.

8. Successive repetitions of a harmonic progression on other pitch levels, or in other keys, is called a _____.

9. Harmonic _____ is a concept that relates both to the distribution of chords in the phrase and to the frequency of chord changes.

10. A balanced pair of phrases is called a _____.

11. A double period is _____
_____

12. A closed form involving two balanced sections is called _____ form.

13. A closed form involving three sections is called _____ form.

Modulation

Words and Ideas

Define in your own words:

static tonality	**modulation**	**background tonality**
modulatory process	**pivot chord**	**intermediate modulation**
tonicize, tonicization	**modulation chain**	**related keys**
parallel scales	**modal mixture**	**shift**
enharmonic changes	**abrupt modulation**	**pivot tones**

SECTION B

Exercises

Psychological Necessity for Change of Key

1. Find three compositions in the Anthology that demonstrate "the static state of tonality." Also, find three additional compositions that reflect "tonality in its dynamic state." List the six titles below.

_____   _____

_____   _____

_____   _____

Elementary Relationships: Three Stages

2. On the staff provided, write the triads that would be suitable for use as pivot chords in a modulation between the two keys designated. Include only chords that are actual triadic members of the keys involved, without invoking secondary dominants, chords from the opposite mode, etc. Label each chord with roman numerals indicating root function in each key ("double analysis").

Example

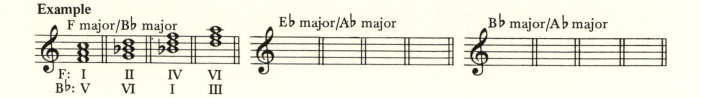

F major/Bb major

F: I   II   IV   VI
Bb: V   VI   I   III

Eb major/Ab major

Bb major/Ab major

G major/D major

F major/G major

F# major/C# major

3. Return to question 2, immediately above, and put an X through any pivot chord that is V of the second key, since this chord generally *is not* used as a pivot chord.

4. In working out modulations involving keys in the minor mode, you should consider all the triads built on the degrees of the harmonic minor scale, together with the variants available from the melodic forms:

Example

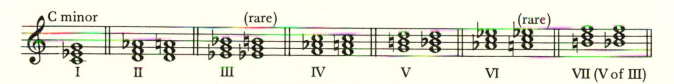

C minor   (rare)   (rare)

I   II   III   IV   V   VI   VII (V of III)

With these in mind, write the potential pivot chords in modulations between the following pairs of keys:

C minor/G minor

G minor/D minor

F major/D minor

E major/F# minor

F minor/Ab major

5. Return to question 4 above, and place an X through all chords that would be interpreted as V in the second key.

Examples of Modulating Phrases

6. Below, write a figured bass that clearly demonstrates a modulation. Be certain that all three stages outlined in your text are worked into these exercises. Begin in D major, and use the I as a pivot to A major.

7. Proceed as in question 6 above, but from C major to A minor, using the pivot chord of your choice.

8. Now use the subdominant chord of B minor as a pivot chord to D major.

9. Now modulate from F major to A minor, using the pivot chord of your choice.

Levels of Tonality: Tonicization and Intermediate Modulation

10. Write a period that modulates by the end of the second phrase, but could return immediately after the confirming cadence to the first key at the beginning of the next phrase.

The Modulation Chain

11. Write a modulation chain in four parts that engages three different keys. Label all chords (double analysis for pivots) and inversions.

Related Keys

12. On the staves below provide key signatures and names of the keys that are considered as near related to the given keys.

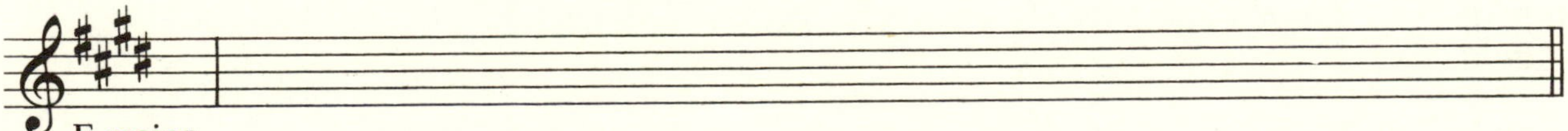

E major

A♭ major

C major

D minor

Interchange of Modes

13. Occasionally a pivot is used that involves a change in mode in one of the keys. For example, in a modulation from D major to B♭ major, the minor IV of D might be used as the VI in B♭. Thus modal interchange provides additional possibilities for pivot chords between two keys. Below, write *only* those pivots that might be obtained from the opposite mode of the first key in each pair.

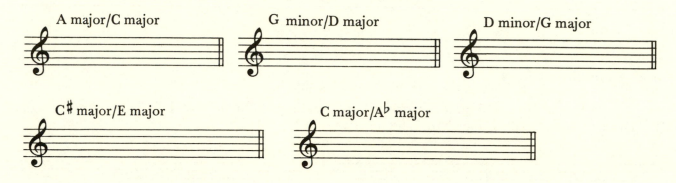

A major/C major   G minor/D major   D minor/G major

C♯ major/E major   C major/A♭ major

Enharmonic Change

14. Because of enharmonic relationships, certain keys may be closely related even though their notation makes them seem distant from each other. For example, C♯ major, seven sharps, and D♭ major, five flats, are really the same key. Give below all potential pivot chords, together with their enharmonic equivalents, between the designated pairs of keys. Label each chord with roman numerals indicating root function in each key.

Example

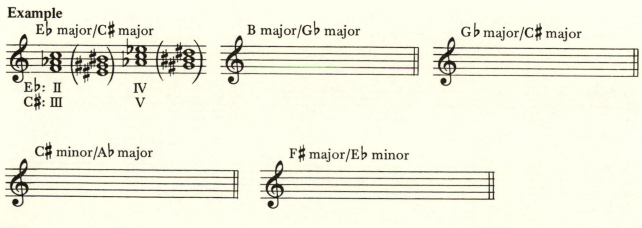

E♭ major/C♯ major   B major/G♭ major   G♭ major/C♯ major

E♭: II   IV
C♯: III   V

C♯ minor/A♭ major   F♯ major/E♭ minor

Analysis

Guidelines for the Observation of Key Structure in Music

I. Observe the initial tonality of the composition. How long does the particular scale prevail?

    a. When do chromatic pitches significantly affect the harmony, suggesting that the state of tonality is in the process of change, or has changed?

    b. At what point are the tonal degrees of the initial key displaced by other tones, in terms of durational, metrical, and other stresses?

    c. Identify the new tonal degrees and the pitch collection or scale from which they are derived. (The point where these are stabilized will necessarily follow any passage where the sense of tonality is interrupted or suspended.)

II. Observe the new tonality. How long does the new scale prevail? (Refer back to 1a and 1b above, as necessary.)

    a. Is the change in the tonality state simply a tonicization? If so, which pitch is tonicized, and for how long?

    b. Is the change an intermediate modulation? What pitch is used as a temporary keynote? What relationship does it bear to the principal tonality, and how many measures are involved?

    c. Is the change a passing or transient modulation or part of a modulation chain? If it is, then determine the keynote of each successive tonality in the chain, along with durations (in terms of numbers of measures) of each.

    d. Is the change a single actual modulation? What is its duration, relative to the initial extent of the old key?

III. Changes in the tonality of a composition often go hand in hand with other form-delineating changes, such as changes in texture or meter, the apparent beginning of a contrasting section, and so forth. Does the change of key in each of the pieces above contribute to the hearing of the composition in well-defined sections? In other words, does the change of key affect your perception of the form of the piece? Give reasons for your answer in each case.

Analyze the key structure of the following pieces from your Anthology. Record the results of your analysis on the score pages.

    a. 2: Bach, Prelude in C major from *The Well-Tempered Clavier*

    b. 13: Corelli, Sonata for Violin and Continuo, Vivace.

    c. 18: Donizetti, Recitative from Scene III of *Betly*

Composition Activities

1. Write an extended melody for solo clarinet consisting of two double periods, that modulates either to the dominant or relative major key, and that modulates back to the original key before ending.
2. Write a duet for flutes with parts of approximately equal interest. Employ several phrases, most of which should be four measures in length, but also some that will demonstrate the means of phrase extension outlined in Chapter 13. About midway in your composition begin a section in the parallel mode, and then modulate to the dominant or to the relative major key. Then modulate again to end in the original tonality and modality.
3. Select a shorter modulating piece from the Anthology. Use this as the basis of an original composition for two trumpets and two trombones. Imitate at least the harmonic progressions and harmonic rhythm, as well as the general key scheme of this model piece.

SECTION E

Self Test

1. When a piece of music employs only notes drawn from a fixed diatonic collection of pitch-classes, it is said to be in a _____ state of tonality.

2. The key scheme, or pattern of keys, in a composition is one of the most significant ingredients of its _____ .

3. There are _____ stages in the mental process of effecting a modulation.

4. It _____ essential that the tonic chord appear for the establishment of a key.
   is/is not

5. A chord common to both keys which will be conveniently susceptible to the change of tonal vantage point is a potential _____ in the modulatory process.

6. Between the keys of G major and D major there are _____ potential pivot chords available.

7. Between the keys of A major and C♯ major there are _____ possible pivot chords.

8. In order to relate keys such as G♭ major and C♯ major, it is necessary to bring into consideration the concept of _____ change or equivalence.

9. The pivot chord chosen is preferably not the _____ of the second key.

10. Establishment of the new key may be confirmed by the introduction of a _____ in that key.

11. Tonicization _____ a genuine modulation.
    constitutes/does not constitute

12. The tonal strength of a tonicization is in direct proportion to the musical _____ through which it extends.

13. When, after confirmation by cadence in the new key, the old key immediately returns, the modulation is called an _____ modulation.

14. Modulations can be only secondary tonal events in a piece beginning and ending in the same key. (True or false?) _____

15. When the modulation from the main key is not followed by an immediate return but by another modulation to a third key, the succession is called a _____ .

16. If two keys have a relatively large number of tones in common, these keys are said to be _____ keys.

17. F♯ major and C♯ major _____ closely related keys.
    are/are not

18. F major and B♭ major _____ closely related keys.
    are/are not

19. Parallel keys, such as B♭ major and B♭ minor, are considered

    _____ .
    only distantly related/practically identical

20. Modal interchange expands the scope of related tonalities available for modulation; most often, modulation involving modal interchange is brought about by borrowing elements of the _____ within the basic context of the _____ mode, rather than vice versa.

21. The use of a C-minor tonic triad by modal interchange in C major _____ afford a convenient pivot in relation to B♭ major.
    would/would not

22. A modulation that sounds sudden or tonally remote is called an _____ modulation.

23. When no real pivot is heard, the instance is best described in terms of _____ rather than modulation.

The Dominant Seventh Chord

Words and Ideas

Define in your own words:

dominant seventh   **harmonic dissonance**   **tendency tones**
unprepared dissonance   **regular resolution**   **dominant six–five**
dominant four–three   **dominant four–two**   **third inversion**
passing chord

Exercises

Origin of the Harmonic Dissonance

1. The following dissonant intervals are taken from V⁷ chords in various keys and positions. Identify each key, name each interval, and show the interval of natural resolution. (Assume that the tonic triad of resolution will be major.)

Example

2. Not all of the following seventh chords are dominant sevenths. Locate those that are dominants and circle them. Indicate the name of the keynote of the scale from which each dominant seventh is derived.

Regular Resolution and Inversions

3. Circle the root of each chord below. (Some of the chords are not V⁷s; change them into V⁷s by adding appropriate accidentals.) Give the names of the key from which each V⁷ is derived.

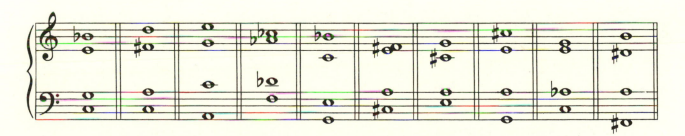

4. Write three different spacings in four parts for each of the following:

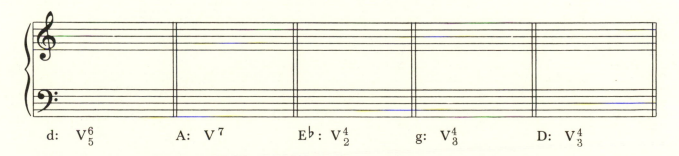

d: V_5^6 A: V^7 E♭: V_2^4 g: V_3^4 D: V_3^4

5. Construct the following dominant sevenths in the positions indicated, and provide regular resolutions for them with the usual voice leading.

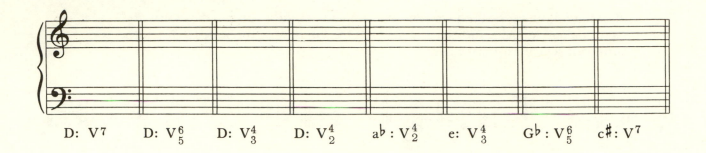

D: V^7 D: V$^6_5$ D: V$^4_3$ D: V$^4_2$ a♭: V$^4_2$ e: V$^4_3$ G♭: V$^6_5$ c♯: V^7

6. Practice constructing dominant sevenths with omitted fifths, in the indicated positions. Resolve regularly.

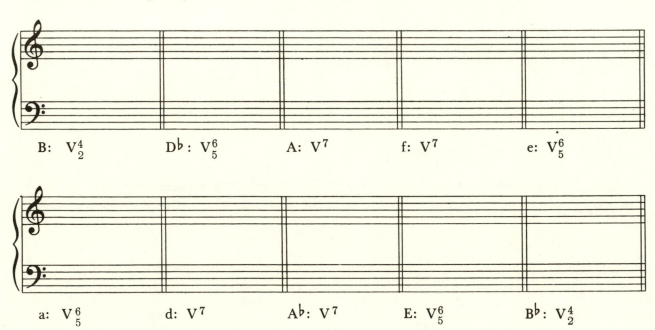

B: V$^4_2$ D♭: V$^6_5$ A: V^7 f: V^7 e: V$^6_5$

a: V$^6_5$ d: V^7 A♭: V^7 E: V$^6_5$ B♭: V$^4_2$

7. In each of the following, place the leading tone of the V^7 in an inner voice; then write a smooth resolution to the tonic, moving the leading tone down to the dominant note.

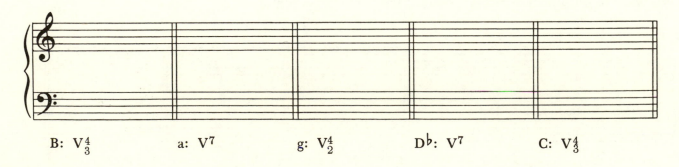

B: V$^4_3$ a: V^7 g: V$^4_2$ D♭: V^7 C: V$^4_3$

8. The following progressions are to be worked out so that the regular resolution of the dominant seventh to the tonic proceeds by irregular voice leading, resulting in the exceptional position or spacing indicated.

134

D: V_3^4 I^6 f: V_3^4 I^6 g: V^7 I^6 F: V^7 I^6 A: V_2^4 I^6 eb: V_2^4 I^6 f#: V_2^4 I G: V_2^4 I

9. Write two different versions of each of the following derived figured bases. Use nonharmonic tones freely.

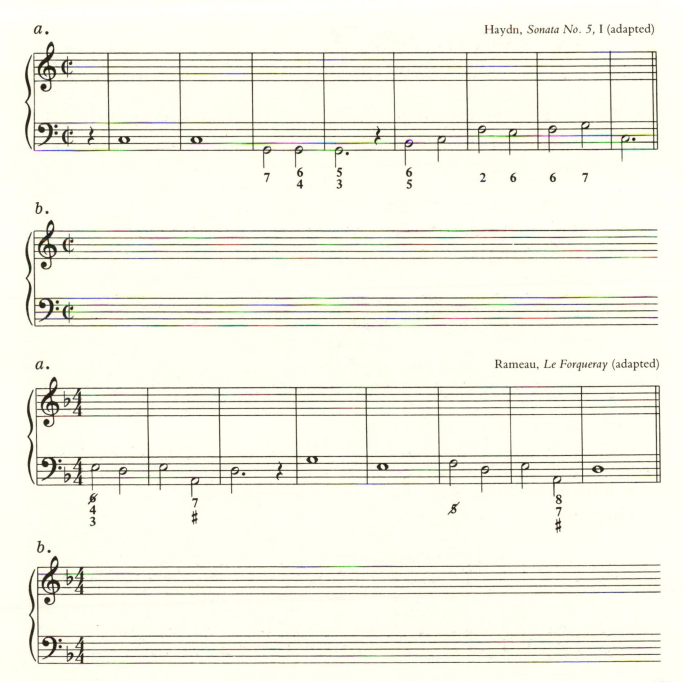

a.

Haydn, *Sonata No. 5,* I (adapted)

b.

a.

Rameau, *Le Forqueray* (adapted)

b.

Analysis

1. The following illustrate the importance of the dominant seventh chord.

a. What is the apparent key of the excerpt above? _____ In what position is the dominant seventh on the first beat of the first full measure? _____ On the second beat? _____

b. What nonharmonic tones can you find in the first full measure? Are there in fact any at all? _____

c. B♭ major has been tonicized in the following excerpt.

Label both chords in relationship to this key.

d. The dominant seventh in the following excerpt suggests that either tonicization or modulation is involved. What temporary tonic is implied in this excerpt? _____ How do you account for the E? _____

e. Label all the chords in the following excerpt in relation to E♭ major. Also identify all nonharmonic tones.

f. In the final example, the principle key of B♭ major is reestablished. Identify the

harmony on the downbeat of the first measure of this excerpt. _____

Identify the harmony in the second half of the same measure. _____

Where does the latter harmony ultimately resolve? _____

What kind of cadential formula is represented by this progression? _____

2. In this example, consider the use of V⁷s and dominant-seventh–like chords (secondary dominant sevenths; see Chapter 16. Label each dominant-seventh type and its chord of resolution. Show voice leading between these chords with connecting dotted lines.

Paganini, *Perpetual Motion*, Op. 11

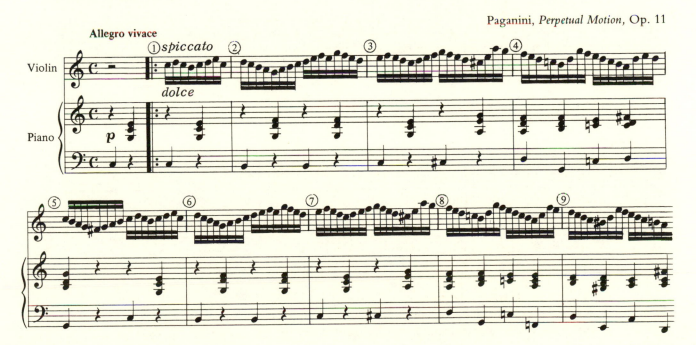

3. Perform the same analysis on the following Anthology pieces. Notate your results on the music itself.

    a. 11: Chopin, *Prelude,* Op. 28, No. 7

    b. 22: Grieg, "The Death of Ase" from the *Peer Gynt Suite,* No. 1

    c. 28: Liszt, *Liebestraume,* No. 3

SECTION D

Composition Activities

1. Write a four-part choral piece based on the harmonic scheme given below, using the meter, tempo, and dynamic level indicated. Make the motion of the piece principally homophonic, that is, with all parts generally moving together.

Chopin, *Prelude,* Op. 28, No. 7 (adapted)

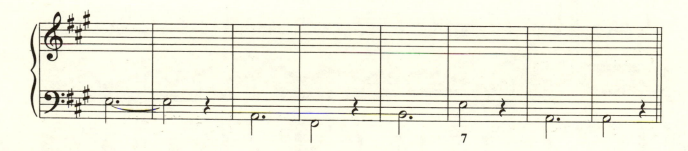

2. Using the same harmonic scheme and bar pattern as in question 1 above, write a short piano piece with a florid melody in the right hand.

Self Test

1. The dominant seventh chord always consists of a _____ third, a _____ fifth, and a _____ seventh, reckoned upward from the root of the chord.

2. Until the dominant seventh chord, the only dissonant chords we have studied are the diminished triads on _____ and _____ in the minor mode and on _____ in the major, and the augmented triad which may be found diatonically in the harmonic minor on the _____ degree.

3. The two dissonant intervals in the root-position dominant seventh chord are the _____ and the _____ .

4. When inverted, these intervals become respectively the _____ and the _____ .

5. Harmonically, the dissonant intervals are followed in their resolutions by _____ intervals.

6. The diminished fifth is most often followed in resolution by a _____ or _____ .

7. In resolution of the dominant-seventh chord, the tendency of the seventh is to _____ .

8. The leading tone in the dominant seventh, when in the upper voice, will most usually move _____ .

9. When in an inner voice in the dominant chord, the leading tone may move up by step to the tonic, or it may move _____ .

10. The augmented fourth on resolution will ordinarily expand to a _____ or _____ .

11. Harmonically speaking, the regular resolution of the dominant seventh chord is to the _____ chord.

12. When a complete dominant seventh chord in root position resolves regularly to the tonic, the chord of resolution is incomplete, having three _____ and a _____ .

13. In the resolution of V^7 to I, preference is _____ shown for the doubling of
    usually/rarely
    tonal degrees in the tonic chord, rather than modal degrees.

14. In an incomplete dominant seventh chord, the factor most likely to be omitted is the _____ of the chord.

15. When the dominant seventh in root position progresses to the first-inversion tonic triad, the seventh of the chord will move _____ so as to avoid doubling the modal third degree in the tonic chord.

16. The last inversion of the dominant seventh chord is called the dominant _____ chord.

17. When an inverted dominant seventh chord resolves, the movement of the leading tone and the seventh _____ generally the same as if the dominant seventh
    is/is not
    chord were in root position.

18. The natural resolution of the dominant four-two is to _____ .

19. The dominant _____ is generally considered as being weaker rhythmically than the other inversions, and is often used as a passing chord between I and I^6; in this regard its function is identical with that of a _____ chord with the seventh present.

The Anthology

CONTENTS

1. JOHANN CHRISTIAN BACH (1735–82)

Two Marches in E♭ major

a. *The Regiment of Prince Ernst*

b. *Husar Regiment of Württemberg*

145

2. JOHANN SEBASTIAN BACH (1685–1750)
Prelude No. 1 from *The Well-Tempered Clavier,*
Book I

3. JOHANN SEBASTIAN BACH
Toccata in D minor

4. JOHANN SEBASTIAN BACH
Chorale: *Sleepers, Awake*

Wake, a - wake, for night is fly - ing, The Watch - man on the
Mid - night hears the wel - come voi - ces, And at the thrill - ing

heights are cry - ing; A - wake Je - ru - sa - lem, at last!
cry re - joi - ces: Come forth, ye vir - gins night is past!

The Bride-groom comes, a - wake, Your lamp with glad - ness take; Al - le - lu - ia!

And for His mar - riage feast pre - pare, For ye must go to meet Him there.

5. LUDWIG VAN BEETHOVEN (1770–1827)

Bagatelle, Opus 33, No. 6

Allegretto
Con una certa espressione parlante

152

6. LUDWIG VAN BEETHOVEN
Sonata in A♭, Opus 26, I, Theme

7. LOUIS BOURGEOIS (ca. 1510–1561)

a. Hymn: *Praise God from Whom All Blessings Flow*

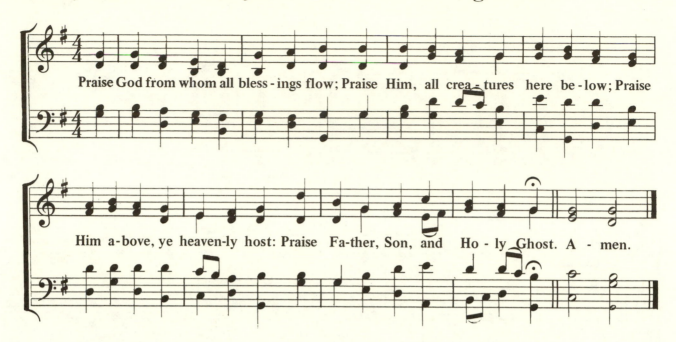

Praise God from whom all bless-ings flow; Praise Him, all crea-tures here be-low; Praise

Him a-bove, ye heaven-ly host: Praise Fa-ther, Son, and Ho-ly Ghost. A - men.

b. Bebop Version of *Praise God from Whom All Blessings Flow*, Andy Jaffe (arr.)

c. Modal Version of *Praise God from Whom All Blessings Flow*, Andy Jaffe (arr.)

8. JOHANNES BRAHMS (1833–97)

Saraband

9. HENRY CAREY (c. 1687–1743)

America

My coun-try, 'tis of thee, Sweet land of lib - er-ty,

Of thee I sing; Land where my

fa - thers died, Land of the Pil - grim's pride, From ev - 'ry

moun - tain side, Let free - dom ring.

10. LUIGI CHERUBINI (1760–1842)

Requiem Mass in C Minor, Sanctus

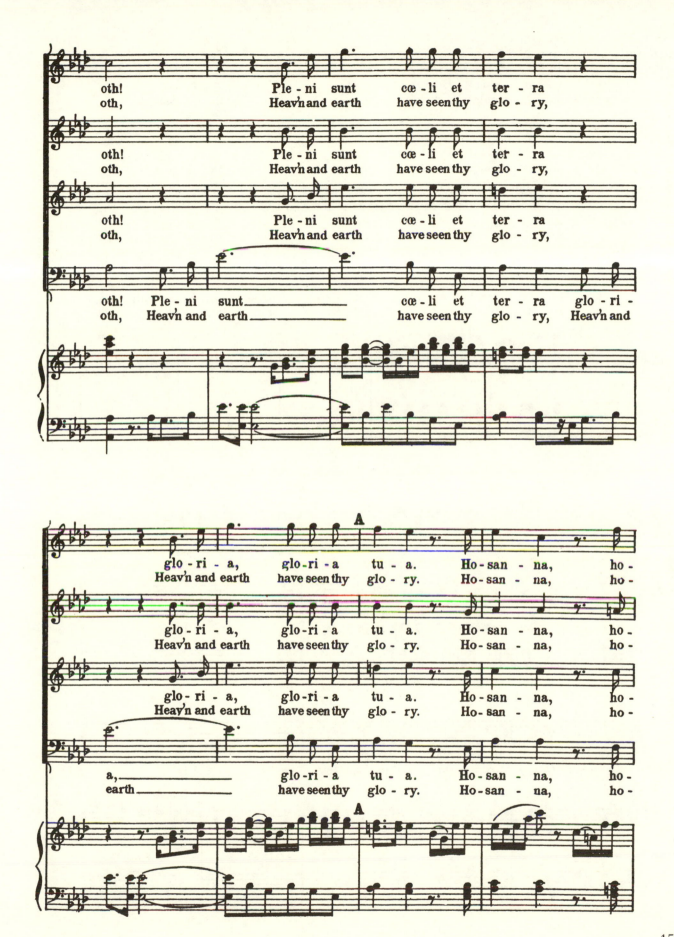

159

11. FRÉDÉRIC CHOPIN (1810–49)
Prelude, Op. 28, No. 7

12. FRÉDÉRIC CHOPIN
Prelude, Op. 28, No. 23

13. ARCANGELO CORELLI (1653–1713)
Sonata for Violin and Continuo, Op. V, No. 4, Vivace

14. FRANÇOIS COUPERIN (1668–1773)

Le Tic-Toc-Choc ou les Maillotins

2ᵉ COUPLET

167

15. LOUIS COUPERIN (c. 1626–61)

a. *Rigaudon* from Suite No. VI

b. *Double du Rigaudon* from Suite No. VI

16. JOHANN CRÜGER (1598–1662)

Hymn: *Now Thank We All Our God*

Adapted by Felix Mendelssohn

1. Now thank we all our God, With heart, and hands, and voic - es,
2. O, may this boun - teous God Thro' all our life be near us,
3. All praise and thanks to God, The Fa - ther, now be giv - en,

Who won - drous things hath done, In whom his world re - joi - ces;
With ev - er joy - ful hearts And bless - ed peace to cheer us;
We wor - ship him who reigns Su - preme in high - est heav - en,

Who from our moth - er's arms Hath blessed us on our way
And keep us in his grace, And guide us when per - plexed,
The one e - ter - nal God, Whom earth and heav'n a - dore;

With count - less gifts of love, And still is ours to - day.
And free us from all ills In this world and the next.
For thus it was, is now, And shall be ev - er - more. A - men.

17. JEAN-FRANÇOIS DANDRIEU (1682–1738)
Magnificat for Organ

18. GAETANO DONIZETTI (1798–1848)

Recitative from *Betly*, Scene III

19. STEPHEN COLLINS FOSTER (1826–64)
Beautiful Dreamer

Moderato.

Beau-ti-ful dream-er, wake un-to me,..... Star-light and dew-drops are wait-ing for thee;..................... Sounds of the rude world heard in the day,............. Lull'd by the moon-light have all pass'd a way!.................

Beau-ti-ful dream-er, queen of my song,......... List while I woo thee with

soft me-lo-dy;............ Gone are the cares of life's bu-sy throng,—

Beau-ti-ful dreamer, a-wake un-to me!.................... Beau-ti-ful dreamer a-wake un-to

me!......................

A Tempo.

Ad Lib.

20. W. S. GILBERT (1836–1911) and ARTHUR SULLIVAN (1842–1900)

Duet: "The Flowers that Bloom in the Spring" from *The Mikado*

that's what we mean when we say, that a thing Is wel come as flow ers that

bloom in the spring. Tra la la la la,— Tra la la la la,— The flow ers that bloom in the

YUM-YUM.

Tra la la la la,— Tra la la la la,— Tra la la la la la la!

PITTI-SING.

Tra la la la la, Tra la la la la, Tra la la la la la la!

spring. Tra la la la la, Tra la la la la, Tra la la la la la la!

POOH-BAH.

Tra la la la la, Tra la la la la, Tra la la la la la la!

21. ALEXANDER GRIBOYEDOV (1795–1829)
Waltz in A♭ major

22. EDVARD GRIEG (1843–1907)

"The Death of Ase" from *Peer Gynt Suite* No. 1

181

23. GEORGE FRIDERIC HANDEL (1685–1759)

Joy to the World

1. Joy to the world! the Lord is come: Let earth re-
2. Joy to the earth! the Sav-iour reigns: Let men their
3. He rules the world with truth and grace, And makes the

ceive her King, Let ev-'ry heart pre-pare him room,
songs em-ploy, While fields and floods, rocks, hills and plains
na-tions prove The glo-ries of his right-eous-ness,

And heav'n and na-ture sing, And heav'n and na-ture
Re-peat the sound-ing joy, Re-peat the sound-ing
And won-ders of his love, And won-ders of his

And heav'n and na-ture sing, And
Re-peat the sound-ing joy, Re-
And won-ders of his love, And

sing, And heav'n, and heav'n and na-ture sing.
joy, Re-peat, re-peat the sound-ing joy.
love, And won-ders, won-ders of his love. A-men.

heav'n and na-ture sing,
peat the sound-ing joy,
won-ders of his love,

24. GEORGE FRIDERIC HANDEL

"He Was Despised" from *Messiah*

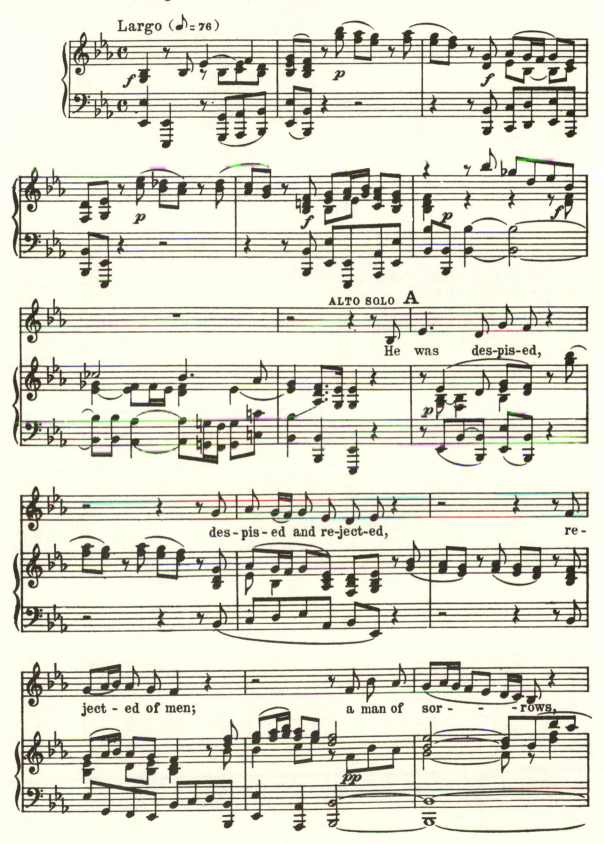

a man of sor - - rows, and ac-quainted with grief, ___

B

___ a man of sor-rows, and ac-quainted with grief.

He

was des-pis-ed, re-ject-ed, He was des-

pis-ed and re-ject-ed of men; a man of sorrows, and acquainted with

grief, _____ a man of sor-rows, and ac-quaint-ed with grief.

He was despis-ed, re-ject-ed; a man of

sorrows, and acquainted with grief, and acquainted with grief, _____

a man of sorrows, and ac-quaint-ed with grief.

187

25. JOSEPH HAYDN (1732–1809)

Der Greis (The Old Man)

Molto Adagio

Soprano: Hin ist al-le meine Kraft, alt und schwach bin ich,

Alto: Hin ist al-le meine Kraft, alt und schwach bin ich,

Tenore: Hin ist al-le meine Kraft, alt und schwach bin

Basso: Hin ist al-le meine Kraft, alt und schwach bin

Pianoforte

we-nig nur er-quik-ket mich, we-nig nur er-quik-ket mich Scherz und Re - ben-

we-nig nur er - quik-ket mich, we-nig nur er - quik-ket mich Scherz und Reben-

ich, we-nig nur er - quik-ket mich, we-nig nur er - quik-ket mich Scherz und Reben-

ich, we-nig nur er - quik-ket mich, we-nig nur er - quik-ket mich Scherz und Reben-

189

26. JOSEPH HAYDN

Twelve German Dances for Two Violins and
Violoncello

No. 2

No. 3

Fine

TRIO

da capo al Fine

No. 4

27. GUSTAV HOLST (1874–1934)

"First Song of the Host of Heaven" from *The Coming of Christ*

Text by John Masefield

To be chanted freely and rather quickly

Men say Pro-me-theus stole the ho-ly fire, And gave it to his fel-lows where they lay Un-der the rock, in win-ter, in the mire; And for his theft he suf-fers Zeus-'s ire, The rock by night, the vul-ture-beak by day, Pangs ev-er-wrench-ing that yet nev-er slay. Now

April snow as-sail the spring;___ So pain at-tends each Chang-er of the Course In which Man feels the sha-dow of God's Wing, Christ is to be Man's Beau-ty and his King, With-in his heart the ev-er-liv-ing source. Not Win-ter's self can stem the Ap-ril's force.

(Sustain this chord
during speech)

28. FRANZ LISZT (1811–86)
Liebestraume No. 3

29. JEAN-BAPTISTE LULLY (1632–87)

"Trompette de L'Opéra," Prelude from the Prologue to *Isis*

Transcribed for Organ

30. WOLFGANG AMADEUS MOZART (1756–91)
Symphony No. 40 in G minor, K. 550, I, Exposition

31. WOLFGANG AMADEUS MOZART

Sonata in A major, K. 331, I, Theme

32. WOLFGANG AMADEUS MOZART
Sonata in D major, K. 284, III, Theme

33. MODEST MUSSORGSKY (1839–91)

Coronation Scene (excerpt) from the Prologue, Scene II, of *Boris Godunov*

To the sun in all splen - dour ris - en be glo - ry, glo -

To the sun in all splen - dour ris - en be glo - ry, glo -

ry, Sing the glo - ry of the Tsar Bo - ris - in Rus - sia, glo - ry!

ry, Sing the glo - ry of the Tsar Bo - ris - in Rus - sia, glo - ry!

(Procession of the Tsar from the cathedral. The police make the people fall in line.)

Bassi.

Long life - and glo - ry!

Tsar, our

Tsar, our

209

34. OLD WELSH AIR

Deck the Halls

1. Deck the halls with boughs of holly,
2. See the blazing yule before us,

Fa la la la la la la la la,

'Tis the season to be jolly,
Strike the harp, and join the chorus,

Fa la la la la la la la la,

Don we now our gay apparel,
Follow me in merry measure,

Fa la la la la la la la la,

Troll the ancient Christmas carol,
While I tell of Christmas treasure,

Fa la la la la la la la la.

35. HENRY PURCELL (1659–95)

Suite No. 1 in G major

Prelude

Almand

Courante

Minuet

36. CAMILLE SAINT-SAËNS (1835–1921)
"The Elephant" from *The Carnival of the Animals*

217

37. ROBERT SCHUMANN (1810–56)

The Poor Orphan Child, No. 6 from *Album for the Young*, Op. 68

38. JOHN PHILIP SOUSA (1854–1932)
The Stars and Stripes Forever

marcato il bassi

222

39. ALICE SPATZ

a. *The Second Farewell* (Bagpipe March)

*If available, use sostenuto pedal throughout.

223

b. *Scarborough Fair* (arr.)

c. Irish Washerwoman (arr.)

d. Motherless Children (arr.)

Moth-er-less chil-dren have a hard — time when their

moth-er's gone. ___ Moth-er-less chil-dren have a hard — time when their

mother's gone._____ They ain't got_ no_ place_ to_ go, you know they

just keep a - wan - der-in' from door__ to door._ Moth-er-less chil - dren have a

hard__ time__ when their moth-er is gone._____

e. *Casi Casi* (arr.)

f. *Off to California* (arr.)

40. JOHANN STAMITZ (1717–57)
Concerto in B♭ major for Clarinet and Orchestra, II

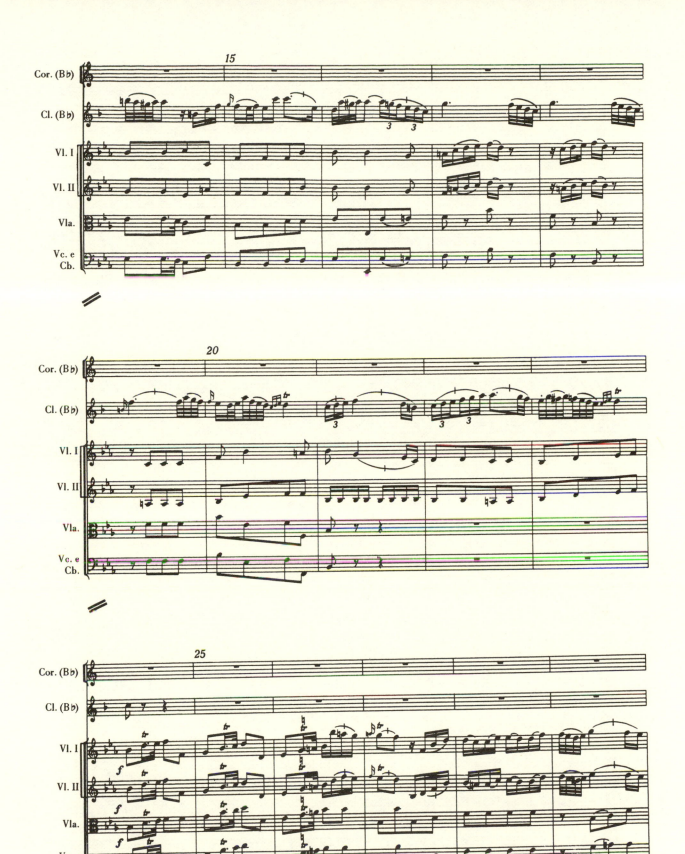

229

230

231

41. STRALSUND SONGBOOK

Hymn: *Praise to the Lord*

42. ROBERT DE VISÉE (ca.1650–ca.1725)

Courante I from Suite III for guitar

43. ANTONIO VIVALDI (1675–1741),
"Summer" from *The Seasons*

E de mosche, e mossoni il Stuol furioso!

235

236

44. JIMMY WEBB (1946–   )

Up, Up and Away

45.

You Deserve a Break Today

Words by Keith Reinhard,
Richard Hazlett & Ed Farran
Music by Sid Woloshin &
Kevin Gavin

Allegro

So much life to be lived,   So much to be tried,

And when you share it you get,   A spec-ial feel-ing in-side,

It's a   full-time thing,   The kind of life that you lead,

A lit-tle break from it all, Is the break that you need.

Slower You de- serve a break to-day, So get up and get a- way to Mc-

Don-ald's, So get up and get a - way to Mc-

Answers to the Self Tests

Unit One: SCALES AND INTERVALS

1. octave
2. seven
3. five
4. whole, whole, half, whole, whole, whole, half
5. tonic
6. tonic, supertonic, mediant, subdominant, dominant, submediant, and leading tone
7. intervals
8. lines and spaces, *or* letter names
9. major
10. melodic
11. harmonic
12. major, minor, augmented, diminished
13. perfect, augmented, diminished
14. compound
15. consonant
16. dissonant
17. perfect unison, perfect octave, perfect fifth, major third, minor third, major sixth, minor sixth, and (sometimes) perfect fourth
18. dissonant
19. dissonant
20. minor
21. diminished
22. perfect
23. second
24. minor sixth
25. enharmonic equivalents
26. F, C, G, D, A, E, and B
27. B, E, A, D, G, C, and F
28. G, D, A, E, B, F♯, and C♯
29. F, B♭, E♭, A♭, D♭, G♭, and C♭

Unit Two: TRIADS

1. chord
2. triad
3. thirds
4. root; third; fifth
5. minor; augmented; diminished
6. major; perfect
7. diminished
8. major third; augmented
9. They are alike in that they both have a perfect fifth; they are different in that the major triad has a major third between root and third, while the minor triad has a minor third.
10. inverted
11. fifth
12. first
13. major; minor
14. augmented; diminished
15. I; IV; V
16. minor
17. diminished
18. is not
19. soprano; alto; tenor; bass
20. doubling
21. root
22. is not
23. larger; smaller

Unit Three: HARMONIC PROGRESSIONS IN THE MAJOR MODE

1. root
2. frequently
3. strong
4. weak
5. common
6. connected
7. "If two triads [to be connected] have one or more tones in common, these *common tones* are usually repeated in the same voice, the remaining voice or voices moving to the nearest tones of the second chord." (Text, p. 26)
8. II–V (when the fourth degree of the scale is the soprano of the II chord)
9. "If the two triads have no tones in common, the upper three voices move in opposite direction to the motion of the bass, but always to the nearest available position." (Text, p. 26)
10. V–VI
11. fifth; triple
12. third; fifth
13. no
14. conjunct
15. skip
16. contrary, oblique, similar
17. true
18. When one voice is moving by step, and the soprano voice, if involved, is not leaping.
19. The interval of augmented fourth, or its inversional equivalent, the diminished fifth, is called the tritone because it is the sum of three whole-tone steps.
20. When two voices move upward in similar motion, the lower voice should not move to a position higher than that just vacated by the upper voice." The corresponding rule holds for descending movement. (Text, p. 35)

Unit Four: THE MINOR MODE

1. F, G, A♭, B♭, C, D♭, E♭
2. relative
3. minor; below
4. minor; above
5. true
6. seventh
7. seventh; higher, or raised
8. third; sixth; lower
9. sixth; seventh; raised
10. no different
11. third
12. 6th, 7th, 7th, 6th
13. harmonic
14. infrequently
15. essentially the same as

Unit Five: TONALITY AND MODALITY

1. tonality
2. modality
3. Dorian; Phrygian; Lydian; Mixolydian
4. may
5. tonic (or keynote)
6. dominant; subdominant
7. I, II, IV, and V
8. C and F
9. III and VI
10. dominant
11. authentic cadence
12. musical words
13. does not
14. major; minor
15. the Picardy third
16. tonicized
17. parallel
18. chromatic

Unit Six: THE FIRST INVERSION—THE FIGURED BASS

1. third
2. 6, or $\frac{6}{3}$
3. roman; arabic
4. I^6
5. second
6. second
7. that the tones a sixth and a third above the bass, or their compounds, are to be sounded
8. the position of the doubled degree in the tonality
9. is not
10. is
11. C
12. are no
13. dominant
14. dominant
15. most often
16. VI
17. leading tone
18. tonic
19. third; fifth; leading tone
20. figured bass
21. that the tone indicated by the numeral is to be chromatically raised
22. that the third (or its compound) above the base is to receive the sign indicated
23. that the note indicated by the figure will be maintained in the harmony until the end of the line, even if the bass changes

Unit Seven: FUNCTION AND STRUCTURE OF MELODY

1. melody
2. countermelody
3. *obbligato*
4. a countermelody in a vocal work which is sung above a principal melody
5. thirds or sixths
6. *cantus firmus*
7. tune
8. development
9. ostinato
10. figuration
11. motive
12. anacrusis
13. phrase
14. cadence
15. antecedent and consequent
16. ornamentation

Unit Eight: NONHARMONIC TONES

1. nonharmonic
2. yes
3. true
4. conjunct
5. consonance
6. resolve
7. stepwise
8. opposite
9. weak
10. appoggiatura
11. anticipation
12. passing tone
13. rhythmically weak
14. "a tone whose natural progression has been rhythmically delayed." (Text, p. 000)
15. appoggiatura
16. escape tone
17. reaching tone
18. escape tone and reaching tone

Unit Nine: THE HARMONIZATION OF A MELODY

1. the same
2. may
3. three
4. are
5. is
6. four
7. is

Unit Ten: THE SIX-FOUR CHORD

1. second
2. fifth
3. perfect fourth
4. an unstable
5. fifth
6. cadential
7. a) it is rhythmically strong with respect to its resolution; b) its fifth is doubled; and c) the other two voices resolve downward by step, like appoggiature
8. downward by step
9. is
10. auxiliary
11. weak
12. a) it is rhythmically weak; b) the bass is stationary with respect to the preceding and following chords; and c) two of the upper voices move as neighbor notes
13. bass
14. I–V$^6_4$–I^6 or the reverse; IV–I$^6_4$–IV^6 or the reverse
15. a) it is rhythmically weak; b) the bass is like a passing tone between two tones belonging to the same harmony; and c) one of the upper voices is like a neighbor note while another upper voice is like a passing tone moving in opposite direction to the bass

Unit Eleven: CADENCES

1. cadences
2. V to I
3. II or IV
4. may
5. strong
6. perfect
7. less
8. half or semicadence
9. IV to I
10. is occasionally
11. deceptive
12. submediant, VI
13. Phrygian

Unit Twelve: HARMONIC RHYTHM

1. root; rhythmic
2. no
3. should
4. nonharmonic
5. need not
6. strength
7. static
8. restlessness
9. static

APPENDIX II

Writing for Instruments—Some Elementary Information

This *Workbook* is based on the assumption that most of you have not studied orchestration or instrumental methods. Yet often in your Composition Activities you are asked to write for instruments that may be unfamiliar to you. In writing for those instruments that your fellow students play, you will be able to learn much from what they can tell you and demonstrate for you. This appendix is provided to get you started on the right track, so you do not write impractical or impossible notes.

Some of the problems in learning to write for instruments are purely mechanical and will disappear with familiarity and practice. Probably the biggest initial difficulty is in transposition, which must be mastered since approximately a third of the orchestral instruments, and more than half of the band instruments, sound pitches different from the notes they read and play. Transposition of instruments is discussed separately in Appendix III.

Other problems are conceptual, and will require you to learn what is instrumentally feasible, to put yourself in the player's mind, as it were. For instance, it is not difficult to learn that the flute is a monophonic instrument and cannot play complete chords the way a piano can; but it is also essential to remember that the flute and all other wind instruments are lung-powered rather than hand-powered, and therefore require rests so that the player can breathe. (As a general rule, the bigger the wind instrument, the more breath will be needed.) Another conceptual problem has to do with qualities of articulation, which differ widely among instruments, yet are part of their very nature; for instance, a slur placed over a succession of notes means a particular kind of articulation for a flute, another for a trombone, still another for a violin; the familiar long slurs stretching over several measures in a piece of piano music are seldom used in writing for winds or strings.

Finally, there is the question of instrumental sound, which is tantamount to saying: "Will it work?" This does not mean "Can it be played?" nearly as much as "Will it sound good?" As you learn to solve the mechanical and conceptual problems, you will come to see that the problems of instrumental sound, whether for single instruments or combined instruments, are the most interesting and challenging of all. It is not for this *Workbook* to begin to meet such challenges, other than to say that your work on the Composition Activities, and the practical realization of them by having them tried out repeatedly, will be excellent preparation for further study in instrumentation. Those of you who become serious composers or orchestrators will always be aware that actually hearing your music will reveal more than any amount of systematic study.

One should begin by learning the ranges of the most familiar instruments. Those given here are considered accessible by average-to-good players; the given notes and all those in between are playable. More advanced students will be able to play somewhat higher, and in the case of most brass instruments somewhat lower as well. For most of the woodwinds, the highest notes are difficult to make sound good; for the brasses, difficult notes at either end of the range are either strident or weak. The tone quality of well-played strings is excellent over nearly the entire range.

It is important to remember that the ranges below include the notes that the instruments can actually *sound.* Instruments marked with a T in parentheses are transposing instruments, which are not notated as they sound (see Appendix III); all others sound as they are written.

Sounding Ranges

Some instruments use more than one clef through their range. The bassoon, trombone, and cello all employ the tenor clef (middle C on the fourth line of the staff) freely in the high register, or, less often, the treble clef. The viola uses the alto clef (middle C on the third line) nearly all the time; most violists would rather read several ledger lines above the alto clef than change to the treble clef for moderately high notes. As a rule, the *8va* sign used everywhere in keyboard music is not congenial to wind and string players, because of fingering differences. A pattern fingered in a certain way on the piano will be fingered identically an octave higher; this is by no means the case in winds and strings. Orchestra players are used to reading *8va,* but generally they find it more comfortable to read extra ledger lines unless these are clearly impractical.

For further reading on this subject, Walter Piston's *Orchestration* (W. W. Norton, 1955) and Samuel Adler's *The Study of Orchestration* (W. W. Norton, 1982) are recommended.

Transposing Instruments

The following summary lists only the transposing instruments likely to be encountered in college music environment. In your study of scores you will from time to time encounter less familiar instruments requiring transposition, such as the *violino piccolo* of Bach's *Brandenburg Concerto No. 1*, or the horns in F♯ in Haydn's *Symphony No. 45*. The various treatises on orchestration will tell you about a good many of these;

but if you master the transpositions of the standard instruments listed here, you will be able to figure out nearly any other kind of transposing instrument on your own.

The following lists are different ways of stating the same kinds of relationships. Choose the one that suits you best.

If you play the following WRITTEN NOTES:

1. on a PICCOLO, it will sound:

2. on an ENGLISH HORN, it will sound:

3. on a CLARINET IN B♭, it will sound:

4. on a CLARINET IN A, it will sound:

5. on a SOPRANINO CLARINET IN E♭, it will sound:

6. on a BASS CLARINET IN B♭, it will sound:

7. on an ALTO SAXOPHONE IN E♭, it will sound:

8. on a TENOR SAXOPHONE IN B♭, it will sound:

9. on a BARITONE SAXOPHONE IN E♭, it will sound:

10. on a HORN IN F, it will sound:

11. on a TRUMPET IN B♭, it will sound:

12. On a DOUBLE BASS if you read:

it will sound:

(The contrabassoon transposes identically.)

Conversely, *if you want to get these sounds:*

1. using a PICCOLO, you won't be able to because they are below the piccolo's range.

2. using an ENGLISH HORN, you will have to write: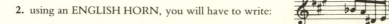

3. using a B♭ CLARINET, you will have to write:

4. using an A CLARINET, you will have to write: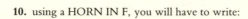

5. using an E♭ SOPRANINO CLARINET, you will have to write:

6. using a B♭ BASS CLARINET, you will have to write:

7. using an E♭ ALTO SAXOPHONE, you will have to write:

8. using a B♭ TENOR SAXOPHONE, you will have to write:

9. using an E♭ BARITONE SAXOPHONE, you have to write:

10. using a HORN IN F, you will have to write:

11. using a TRUMPET IN B♭, you will have to write: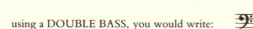

12. If you wanted the following:

using a DOUBLE BASS, you would write:

Stating these rules in words instead of examples:

1. The piccolo sounds one octave above the written notes.

2. The English horn sounds a perfect fifth below the written notes.

3. The B♭ clarinet sounds a major second below the written notes.

4. The A clarinet sounds a minor third below the written notes.

5. The E♭ sopranino clarinet sounds a minor third above the written notes.

6. The B♭ bass clarinet sounds an octave and a major second below the written notes (an octave below the ordinary B♭ clarinet).

7. The E♭ alto saxophone sounds a major sixth below the written notes.

8. The B♭ tenor saxophone sounds an octave and a major second below the written notes (i.e., just like the bass clarinet).

9. The E♭ baritone saxophone sounds an octave and a major sixth below the written notes (an octave below the alto saxophone).

246

10. The horn in F sounds a perfect fifth below the written notes (i.e., just like the English horn).

11. The trumpet in B♭ sounds a major second below the written notes (just like the ordinary B♭ clarinet).

12. The double bass sounds a perfect octave below the written notes (so does the contrabassoon).

Or to put it another way:

1. Write the part for the piccolo one octave lower than you want it to sound.

2. Write the part for English horn a perfect fifth higher than you want it to sound.

3. Write the part for B♭ clarinet a major second higher than you want it to sound.

4. Write the part for A clarinet a minor third higher than you want it to sound.

5. Write the part for E♭ sopranino clarinet a minor third lower than you want it to sound.

6. Write the part for B♭ bass clarinet an octave and a major second higher than you want it to sound.

7. Write the part for E♭ alto saxophone a major sixth higher than you want it to sound.

8. Write the part for B♭ tenor saxophone an octave and a major second higher than you want it to sound.

9. Write the part for E♭ baritone saxophone an octave and a major sixth higher than you want it to sound.

10. Write the part for horn in F a perfect fifth higher than you want it to sound.

11. Write the part for trumpet in B♭ a major second higher than you want it to sound.

12. Write the part for double bass an octave higher than you want it to sound.